Body Consciousness

Body Consciousness

SEYMOUR FISHER

Jason Aronson   *New York*

Library of Congress Cataloging in Publication Data

FISHER, SEYMOUR.
    Body consciousness.

    Bibliography: p.
    1. Body image. I. Title. [DNLM: 1. Body image—Popular
works. 2. Personality—Popular works. BF 697 F536b 1973]
BF697.F484   152
ISBN: 0-87668-181-X
LC: 74-18899

First Aronson Edition 1974
Preface 1974 Jason Aronson, Inc., New York
    1973 by Prentice-Hall, Inc.
Originally published as *Body Consciousness: You Are What You
Feel*

To my wife, who urged me to write this book

Contents

Preface

Human behavior is too often translated into depersonalized abstractions. Our major personality theories abound with explanatory concepts like "ego," "drive," and "identity" which, in their detachment, give little hint that they deal with events occurring in people with living, breathing bodies. The person who feels anxious or disturbed obviously is confronted with something more than "anxiety." He experiences a great mass of sensations that are anchored in his body and that shift along gradients of intensity and discomfort. The patient in psychotherapy whose therapist suddenly confronts him with an incisive interpretation experiences the event, and gives meaning to it, in the context of a rich network of body feelings. The schizophrenic suffering his first acute episode is immersed with his whole body in the disorganizing process. It is happening to all of him. This book was written to call attention to the importance of such experience, not only in the disturbed but also normal individual's reactions to the world. A considerable fund of scientific information has accumulated in this area which is ripe for communication and practical application.

Our stream of body experience is so constantly with us that we take it for granted and fail to recognize either its complexity or the dramatic ways in which it transforms our perspectives. We do, in fact, live within the confines of a body image or body concept that functions to structure and give stability to our psychological world. Our body perceptions constitute a core of self-definition and provide the compass points for self-orientation. We are most vividly reminded of the fundamental functions of our body concept when we encounter examples of its distruption in various pathological states. The brain-damaged individual who loses the ability to distinguish right from left portrays the central import of the body concept in giving spatial directionality to our environs. A schizophrenic patient who delusionally concludes that his body is split in half and that he is simultaneously two different people reminds us that the normal individual accomplishes a difficult task in learning to integrate the experience he has with his bilaterally duplicated self-representation. An individual who begins to feel, under the impact of a dose of LSD, that his body is breaking out of its usual limits and merging with other objects highlights the fact that we unthinkingly accept in our normal state the ability we have acquired to define our body boundaries precisely and to maintain a clear idea of our demarcation from the milieu in contact with us. Any clinician who deals with the psychologically disturbed will repeatedly encounter complaints that reflect distortions in the body image. Patients will variously mention feelings of depersonalization, persistent aggravating sensations in specific body areas, and concern about the inadequate size of important body organs. The educator too must deal with problems that relate to body feelings. He is confronted by students who are puzzled by the emphasis the school puts on the importance of the head and the brain as compared with the other sectors of the body. He has to face complaints that grow out of the discomforts of keeping one's body inactive and nonmobile for long periods of time in the classroom. To understand body-based complaints one must grasp the way in which the individual builds up a map of his body, assigns meaning to it, and uses it as a screen upon which to project his anxieties.

You are faced with an enormously difficult task as you try to understand your own body psychologically. Myriads of questions arise about your body: Why am I so hyperaware of a certain body part? Why do I feel ashamed of another part? Why am I afraid that my body will get hurt? Why do I have persistent unpleasant feelings about a particular body locale? Why do some of my body organs feel abnormally large or small? What should I do about body feelings that don't make sense and keep intruding into my thoughts? Do I appear to others the way I see myself in the mirror?

It has become clear that learning to understand and give meaning to what is witnessed "in my body" is a task that compares in toughness with that of an explorer who finds himself in a new territory of complex terrain and tries to conjure up a map of it all. In some ways the task of understanding your own body is of even greater magnitude. The explorer has been taught systematic techniques for charting new territories. There are no such explicit techniques taught in our culture about "body mapping." While the child is given arduous training in how to master words, numbers, space, and even social relationships, little, if anything, is ever said to him about systematically comprehending the events in his own body. Aside from injunctions related to eating, sphincter control, being ill, and "looking good" he is not really given more than a few whispered hints about all of the other things he witnesses in his "body world."

The child, in mapping his own body, is also severely hindered by the strange set of rules that he must follow as he goes about it. The peculiarity of these rules can best be conveyed by applying them to the task of the explorer. Imagine an explorer who wanders into unknown territory and who then prepares to construct a map of its contours. If he were burdened by the same game-playing rules as the average individual in our culture who wants to gain an understanding of his own body experiences, he would have to proceed in the following handicapped condition: First of all, he would not be able to scrutinize parts of the territory because it would be somehow reprehensible to do so; even after making observations he would not be able to express some of them in explicit, acceptable words or symbols—rather he would have to fall back on a taboo language, whose use is frowned upon; finally, the distorted map that he might eventually produce would have to be kept secret and rarely, if ever, shown to anyone else.

Because the average person has so much difficulty in developing a clear, meaningful map of his body, it remains a rather mysterious place to him. This very mystery encourages him to think about body processes less rationally than he usually thinks about his daily affairs. It pushes him to relate to his own body in the anxious, semisuperstitious way in which he deals with anything that is vitally important but poorly understood. You need not go any further than the nearest television or movie screen to find mirrored the rather childlike, alarmed attitude that the average person takes toward his body. Much of the content that passes across such screens concerns the strange and destructive transformations that can befall the body. There is, for example, a fascinated preoccupation with monsters whose faces and bodies are hideously distorted. Often the monsters are ordinary people who unkowningly ingested a bad substance or were exposed to some potent new force. Implicit in such themes is the idea that one's body is capable of peculiar alterations—that we are all potential Frankenstein figures. The preoccupation with body anxiety is exemplified, too, in repetitious television accounts of characters who have strange diseases or who require radical medical treatment if they are to survive.

Everywhere there is evidence that people evolve a repertoire of weird ideas about body events. They keep wondering whether their body experiences are normal or deviant. Is it normal to feel suddenly that a part of your body does not belong to you? How peculiar is it that you have the sensation that your head is larger than it should be? Because there is so much mystery about the body, people do not know how to answer such questions and usually end up feeling a bit panicked when confronted by what appear to be "strange" sensations. In actual fact, there is good research evidence (Fisher, 1970) that perceiving a part of one's body for brief periods as foreign ("not mine") is a normal occurrence and not at all a cause for alarm. This "depersonalization" of one's body is abundantly common in people who are coping with difficult or stressful conditions. The anxiety generated by poorly understood body experiences incites people to all kinds of compensatory, self-protective maneuvers, which often eventuate in their doing strange things to their own bodies. They are defensively driven to camouflage and reshape their frames in an effort to hide from themselves and others body feelings that are threatening. There is no end to the body-camouflage techniques that have been dreamed up. They range from relatively minor defenses represented by wearing wigs, padded bras, and elevator shoes to more radical defenses exemplified by breast augmentation surgery, tattooing, and genital alteration (penis amputation, for example). They also range from the obvious, as in actually altering the appearance of regions of the body, to the more concealed, as in psychologically rejecting the existence of certain body organs or in the habitual touching of areas that the individual has a need to highlight. It is difficult to think of any human enterprise to which greater quantities of effort, money, and ingenuity are devoted than that involved in converting one's body into an acceptable and understandable companion.

The notion that Napoleon was drawn to world conquest because of his inferior stature is a fanciful myth, but it contains the core of an idea that is probably valid and has more than passing significance. There is trustworthy evidence that body attitudes affect the way people act in the nonbody world "out there." Research findings (Fisher, 1970) indicate that body attitudes may play various roles—in how closely and comfortably an individual gets along with others, in how daring he is, in his preferences for certain kinds of sexual stimulation, and in his response to becoming ill or crippled. Aside from obvious instances—such as when a headache or stomach pain turns an individual irritable and causes him to act unfriendly toward others—there seem to be other channels through which body attitudes are manifested. Considerably more will be said about this matter at a later point. There are studies which indicate that body feelings are projected onto the world, that the individual can ascribe to people and things feelings that simply mirror how he perceives his body. Thus, a person who doubts the strength and integrity of his body may express this feeling by being chronically afraid that intruders will break into his house (or perhaps even that the borders of his country will be invaded). Or an individual who needs persistent stimulation of one localized body sector (mouth or genitals, for example) to feel secure may irrationally pursue certain activities that will provide such stimulation. Apropos of this last example, Chessick (1960) describes the importance the drug addict attaches to his favorite drug, producing a high level of arousal in one or more specific areas of his body. He calls this kind of highly arousing and motivating body experience in the addict "pharmacogenic orgasm."

Turning in a personal direction, I would like to say that the essays dealing with body experience in this book represent a long-standing ambition on my part to apply what is scientifically known about body image and body feelings to a variety of contemporary issues. I have been involved in the writing of two previous scientific monographs (Fisher and Cleveland, 1968; Fisher, 1970) and numerous research papers concerned with body experience. These works were expressed in the careful, constrained language of scientific custom. But I have felt for some time that it would be interesting to adopt the existing framework of available information about body experience as a prism through which various problems could be viewed in a broader, more speculative manner. It seemed to me to be a promising exercise to apply our understanding of body attitudes to clarifying such matters as male-female differences; current modes of exciting, drugging, and clothing the body; prejudice against blacks and Jews; styles in the artistic world; the ways in which we use and misuse space in our homes, vehicles, and cities; and our struggles against illness and the threat of death.

Let me explain more specifically the plan of this book. I have sifted the literature concerned with body experience and reduced it to eight major themes, each of which is taken up in a separate chapter. This material will provide the reader with an overview of where we stand in our understanding of the body as a personal, psychological event. Within each chapter I have described a particular aspect of body experience, then considered the multiple strategies that the individual uses in making sense of it, and finally explored in depth how these strategies in turn affect his style of behavior. I have tried in each instance to trace a connection between a certain form of body feelings and a parallel life attitude or dilemma. For example, one chapter considers the link between an individual's race prejudice and his doubt concerning the stability of his body. Another reviews the part that sensitivity to body feelings plays in the ability to be creative. Still another appraises how an individual's attitudes toward his body size can affect his concepts of space and distance. Throughout, there is exploration of how body feelings affect one's ability to cope with psychological conflict and stress. I have aimed at presenting a general frame of reference for interpreting a wide variety of behaviors that have their origin in body attitudes and feelings.

CHAPTER ONE

Why is it difficult to know your own body?

If you walk into a room in which there is a mirror of whose existence you are unaware and you are unexpectedly confronted by your own image, the chances are that you will momentarily feel that you are face to face with an unknown, somehow alien person. Freud (1924) described such an experience. He reported:

> I was sitting alone in a compartment of a sleeping car when a violent jolt opened the door of the adjoining washroom and an aged man, wearing a dressing gown and a cap, entered my compartment. I supposed that he had mistaken his direction when leaving the washroom, which was situated between two compartments. I arose to so inform him, when I was stupefied by recognizing that the intruder was myself reflected by the mirror in the washroom door.

Similarly, Wolff (1943) was able to show that a person has a difficult time identifying pictures of his own hands or even his own profile when he is not expecting to be confronted by them. If, without a person's knowledge, you take a picture of his profile (in silhouette form) and you later present this picture among a series of pictures of other persons' profiles, he will almost invariably be unaware that he is looking at a representation of himself. This is a well-documented fact.

A variety of similar observations have been made. For example, people have difficulty in visualizing accurately the size of certain parts of their bodies. They are especially likely to overestimate their head dimensions (Wapner, 1960). The head "feels" larger than it actually is. Similarly, investigators at one institute (Traub and Orbach, 1964) have reported that if you put a person in front of a special mirror that has been cleverly designed so that it can systematically distort his image and if he is shown how to manipulate the controls of this mirror, he has great difficulty in converting the distorted reflection back to his true image. He has trouble "remembering" what he does, in fact, look like.

The more that one thinks about this and other phenomena—such as the alien quality of one's unexpectedly encountered mirror image—the more puzzling and paradoxical are the implications. After all, there are few, if any, other objects in his environment with which the individual is more acquainted than his own body. He sees his body every day and spends an uncountable number of seconds touching, smelling, and receiving impressions from it. Presumably he should know his body in a uniquely detailed and intimately precise fashion. It would be misleading, of course, to deny that the average individual does accumulate a good deal of intimate detail about his own body, but despite this fact he seems to have formidable blind spots with respect to it—and remains remarkably unsure and puzzled about its properties.

Why should this be so? One of the simplest and most obvious reasons is that our bodies are constantly changing and there is often a time lag in bringing our body concepts up to date. The rapidly changing adolescent girl may hold on to a picture of her body as it was before her breasts became prominent. The aging woman may remember herself as she was before her skin lost its elasticity. Some observations I made while interviewing persons who had been blind for varying periods of time are relevant to this situation. One man, who at the time of our interview was well into his middle years but who had lost his sight at the age of ten, told me that when he thought about himself he seemed to possess the same physical attributes that he had years previously when he could see himself in the mirror. Despite the fact that he had grossly altered in physique since childhood (and he was, of course, clearly aware of this fact from the responses of others and also from his own tactile and kinesthetic sensations), he had only the ten-year-old visual image in his memory repertoire.

So far as visual imagery was concerned, he could think of his body only in the little-boy way it had appeared years earlier. This is a unique state of affairs, but in its extreme form it illustrates what commonly occurs to a lesser degree in other persons.

Another example of the body concept's resistance to alteration is encountered in those who suffer the amputation of some part of the body like an arm or leg (or nose, breast, penis). It is quite normal following such amputation to continue to experience the absent part as if it were still there. This is referred to as the "phantom limb" phenomenon. The amputee may vividly feel that he still retains the lost body part. He may be so convinced of the reality of a nonexistent leg that upon awakening in the morning he will attempt to stand upon it and fall flat. Some have interpreted the "phantom" as an expression of time lag or of the individual's resistance to recognizing a radical shift in his body. He seems to want to "hold on" to his body as it was and resists revising his image of it. Similarly, in a milder way, the average person may not know his current body as well as he should because he is "holding on" to a more or less out-of-date version.

There may be other, perhaps even more important, reasons why people find it so difficult to develop a realistic "body picture." One that should be especially highlighted is related to the difficulties the average individual has in taking a long hard look at his own body and really seeing it as it is. First of all, it is literally not easy to get a look at a number of important body sectors. There is the fundamental fact that most of the time your body is covered by concealing and sometimes deceptive clothing. Furthermore, it requires an elaborate assemblage of mirrors to get a clear view of the back of your body. Even profile views require a special mirror setup that the average individual rarely has available. The genitals, which are certainly a prime center of interest for most persons, are extremely difficult to examine visually. Without a mirror the male can only see limited aspects of his penis and testicles. The female can, in actuality, see almost nothing of her genital structures; she certainly cannot see the vagina. Of course, neither sex can see the anus. It is probable that the average individual arranges to look at his genitals or anus in a mirror on only a relatively few occasions. It should be added, despite its obviousness, that there is no opportunity to inspect visually what goes on within the interior of your body. The whole complex interior is out of sight.

There is a gross vagueness in the average person's perception and understanding of the inside of his body. Investigators (Tait and Ascher, 1955) who developed a test that was based on asking people to draw a picture of the inside of the body found widespread ignorance of the facts. People seem to have only the vaguest notions of what organs reside within themselves and the spatial interrelationships of these organs. Interviewers (Nagy, 1953; Gellert, 1962, for example) who have painstakingly questioned young children about their knowledge of the inside of the body have found that it is fragmentary. They have a few simple notions—that the inside is like a container and that it is a place "where the food goes."

All of this adds up to the slightly surprising fact that most people do not, because of purely practical limitations, get a chance to look carefully or for extended periods at major sectors of their body geography. True, other kinds of sensations (touch, pain, temperature) emanate abundantly from the "hidden" body areas, but they do not offer anywhere near the sharpness of definition provided by visual inspection.

Even when a person has the opportunity to take a good look at his body, he does so through an elaborate set of selective filters and screens. There are observations in the literature that suggest that if people look at themselves strong emotions are aroused, some of which are inhibitory. Feelings of guilt and shame and others of an unpleasant variety may be elicited that produce avoidance reactions. The individual may find it unpleasant to gaze upon his own image and therefore defensively "looks away" or puts little energy into his scrutiny.

The difference between just superficially looking at yourself and *really* doing so is poignantly illustrated by an account given by Fisher (1958). He describes the case of a badly crippled woman who had made an adequate adjustment to her distorted body until one day she viewed a film that a friend had made of her walking along. Although she had seen her crippled body many times in the mirror, the image that was conveyed by the non-censoring camera was so overwhelmingly ugly and grotesque that she was deeply shocked and subsequently, as part of her reaction, developed depressive symptoms. Just as this woman had never allowed herself to glimpse her true body appearance, the average person probably "keeps his distance" when viewing himself.

One significant component of the negative feeling about one's body derives from the negative attitude toward body events in most religious and moralistic systems. Another is the disrepute into which the body has fallen as an object of worth as the result of its decreasing importance as a source of energy. For centuries there has been a rolling campaign against the body realm. Man has been made to feel that his body is not only dirty and bad but also powerless and useless. The saga of the "dirty body" is too well known to require review. Religious and other moralistic agents have portrayed the body as a source of sin and preached that the child must learn early of the dangers lurking beneath his skin and be provided with techniques for mastering them. He has had to avoid touching himself without good reason, to defecate in a special ceremonial fashion, and generally to evade making decisions on the basis of body feelings. The culture tells each individual as he is growing up that he has to master the irrationality of his body —by covering it up, putting it on a schedule, and listening to what it has to say only at certain "right" times. Parallel with this badness theme, which now is diminished in its religious form but still flourishes in doctrines that emphasize rationality and intellectuality (and which assume that the only good part of the body is the head), there has been a trend toward substituting machines for muscles and by so doing downgrading the worth of the body. The number of human activities in which moving muscles can produce a profit or gain a man honor is steadily diminishing. The message is vividly communicated that a man's body is worth less and less as a tool or a means of achieving success. This means that his body is assigned less value and he has greater difficulty in taking pride in his body. Except for certain positive attitudes toward the bodies of the beautiful woman and the athletically skillful man (which are usually expressed in terms of ideals that many people cannot attain), the body is generally not an admired object in our culture. There are a lot of things that happen and a lot of things we are told while growing up that dampen our enthusiasm about closely perusing our own bodies.

As an aside, it is interesting to consider how few legitimate occasions you have for carefully scrutinizing your own body. The times are rare when it is "officially" all right with parents or the establishment to examine your own body feelings in minute detail. One of these times is when you are sick, about to become sick, or are consulting a physician; then it is acceptable to mull over your body sensations. Of course, even in this context the emphasis is upon whether the sensations that are experienced are normal or abnormal. The child soon learns that his parents do not want him to say much explicitly about his body unless it concerns the possibility of illness. A child who otherwise launches into detailed descriptions of his body feelings to his parents is likely to be regarded as odd. Eventually the child learns to associate body awareness with matters of health and illness. In fact, he may even avoid scanning his body because he is afraid that it might turn up clues of impending illness. The whole matter of perceiving his body gets irrationally enmeshed with the sick role. Sick people may focus awareness on their bodies, but well people should not. If you want to scrutinize your body attentively you first have to get yourself certified as "sick." By isolating intensive analysis of one's body sensations in the realm of medical pathology, the whole process of body awareness is given negative connotations. As will be seen, this is especially true in the case of men; and less so for women. At a more general level, one can say that in our culture the careful analysis of body experiences (in the form of reported symptoms) has been left almost entirely to the physician. Poets, dancers, artists, psychotherapists, and chiropractors have also taken a fair amount of interest in such experiences—but only unofficially and under a vague cloud of suspicion. Paradoxically, the most successful in this area is the chronic hypochondriac. Although at a great psychic cost, he creates a way of life for himself in which he can be endlessly preoccupied with his body sensations.

The superstitious way in which we come to interpret body events is unhappily illustrated by what has been found in studies of children who suffer serious body disability. A basic reaction in such children is one of guilt. A young child who had a leg amputated clearly verbalized the idea that he must have done something bad to have such a terrible thing happen to him. This is true not only of children. Adults who have suffered gross body damage reveal, if one wins their confidence, similar guilty thoughts. There are tremendous injections of guilt contained in our current modes of teaching the child about his body. Almost everything that we tell him is phrased in terms of "don't" and "that is bad." He receives endless prohibitions against being too dirty, not properly controlling his sphincters, and not maintaining a sufficiently attractive appearance. There is also a powerful tendency for parents to make children feel "bad" about being physically ill. When a child becomes sick, this is a threat and an inconvenience to the parents. It means extra work and worry for them. No matter how altruistic and properly parental they are, they are likely to be annoyed and even downright angry—especially if an illness of any duration is involved. They indirectly convey to the child that when he is sick he is making things tough for them. It is therefore not surprising that he begins to feel that any breakdown in his body functioning has the potential of making his parents suffer and also making them angry at him. This view is reinforced by the fact that children soon learn that illness is a nice tempting way to avoid responsibility. If you don't feel like going to school, an acute stomach ache might rescue you for the day. Parents quickly become suspicious of such body tactics and may initially look upon any physical complaint by the child as a devious attempt to get out of what is expected of him. The child's body becomes a pawn in a variety of power games that he plays his parents. It should be added that a parent is disturbed by his child's illness not only because it inconveniences him but also because of his close identification with his body. For a long time the parent feels that his child's body belongs to him, and in some ways he does not really distinguish his child's body from his own. His underlying feeling might be paraphrased as "What happens to you happens to me," so when the child becomes ill his unique closeness to him easily arouses threatening anxiety at the level of "This could happen to me" or "This is almost happening to me." What has just been said is not mere speculation. Two investigators (Centers and Centers, 1963) actually found that parents of deformed children seem to be much more identified with their children's bodies than are parents of healthy children. There is also the interesting complementary observation (Arnaud, 1959) that children raised in a family where one of the parents has some serious body defect are unusually anxious about their bodies. One would guess that they too identify closely with the body of the sick parent.

Quite speculatively, I would propose that man avoids a dispassionate appraisal of his own mirror image because he sees too much in it that is disquieting. He perceives long imprinted facial expressions, favorite body postures, and styles of self-adornment that remind him of crises and painful emotional conflicts he has endured. The tight lines around his mouth may "recall" his chronic struggles to hold back the angry words he would like to have vented on his father or other authority figures. The stiff way he holds his body may evoke an awareness of the fact that he habitually adopts the alert stance of someone prepared for imminent danger. While this idea is speculative, it fits in with observations by Holzman and his coworkers (1966), who concluded that people are so often disturbed when listening to tape recordings of their own voices because the intonations and expressive styles they detect are imprints of attitudes and intents they adopted toward life that have bad, ego-alien implications. An individual listening to his own tape-recorded voice may sense childishly dependent or angry or sexual communications in its sound quality that he had long denied in himself.

Finally, I would like to hypothesize that there is resistance to looking directly and naively at your own body because in so doing its properties as a *concrete* object become too painfully obvious. Most people do not think of their bodies as biological things that consist of matter like any other things they encounter from day to day. They equate their bodies with elaborate concepts of selfhood and endow them with very special (superior to other objects) properties. There is comfort in thinking of your body not as a mere physical object, which, as such, would be subject to all of the vicissitudes and happenings that befall ordinary objects in the universe. But if an individual inspects his body without reservation he must necessarily perceive that it is basically a biological phenomenon like all other biological organisms. Ultimately, it is a collection of matter, regardless of how complex the values and meanings ascribed to it. To become aware of this fact is to open the door to intimations of mortality and other forms of vulnerability. It is probably important defensively to most people to conceptualize their bodies within an elaborate framework of psychological meaning that functions almost like a halo or protective armoring— denying that the body is, after all, an aggregate of molecules not much different from those occurring widely in nature. It is difficult for man to accept that his body is not "above" it all. The everlasting appeal of religious doctrines of immortality bears witness to this fact.

Man's puzzlement about his body is sometimes dramatically reflected in the behavior of those who are psychotic. Rosenzweig and Shakow (1937) set up a mirror in a room and, from a concealed position, watched how schizophrenic patients acted when they were alone in the room. They reported that these patients would often stand directly in front of the mirror and stare with continued fascination at their own images. They would also make faces, as if testing to see how such behavior would "look" in the mirror image. There are different perspectives that one can adopt in interpreting this kind of mirror behavior, but I would favor the view that it represents curiosity about something that has long been mysterious. The schizophrenic, having lost some of his inhibitions and controls, seeks openly to find in the mirror a clearer picture of the body world that has probably never made sense to him. He acts out uninhibitedly what the average person must from time to time yearn to do—that is, to make a deep, unashamed perusal of himself. This same body curiosity is evidenced by some schizophrenics who "poke around" in taboo body openings like the anus, inserting objects and apparently experimenting with different kinds of sensations that are manipulatively aroused. One wonders, too, whether the excited schizophrenic woman who suddenly throws off her clothes and exposes herself is not, among other aims, trying to make contact with the world of her own body that has previously been hidden or denied to her direct awareness.

The secrecy surrounding the body makes it difficult for the average individual to judge what it *should* "feel" like. He lacks publicly stated norms against which he can match his own experiences. If he wonders whether his body is seriously deviant in some way or if he is uncertain as to whether it is somehow not "right," he may be driven to extreme measures to get information that will help him to allay his painful puzzlement. A relevant example is the male exhibitionist who compulsively displays his penis to women in public places. Various explanations have been offered for this odd pattern of behavior, but many of them can be reduced to the idea that the exhibitionist is looking for information about his penis. He studies the reactions of those to whom he shows his penis and tries to deduce how they regard it. He may be seeking information as to whether they perceive it as being as inferior as it "feels" to him, or whether they perceive it as being as bad or dirty as it "feels" to him. It is of parallel interest that Kernaleguen (1968) found that women on college campuses who adopt the latest clothing fashions (and exhibit themselves in these fashions) are those who experience their bodies as particularly vulnerable and open to invasion. Is it possible that they, too, are especially motivated to get others to look at their bodies so that they can monitor their reactions and deduce whether these reactions do or do not support their inner feelings of body inferiority? In other words, the campus fashion leader may look to see if her inner alarm about her body is justified by the reactions of others who have been invited to look at her. The camouflage intent in wearing the latest fashions is also obvious, of course, and will be discussed in more detail in a later chapter. It is not too farfetched to speculate that many persons who seem to be dedicated to getting into the public spotlight may unconsciously be seeking reassuring information about their bodies, as it is conveyed in the responses of others to the sight of them. The actor, the dancer, the strip teaser, and perhaps even the politician may be looking for an elemental kind of body reassurance. As far as that goes, there are times when we all invite others to give us feedback about how our bodies appear to them. Our self-consciousness when we wear a new item of clothing may unconsciously cajole others to look at us and to register a reaction, for or against. Laing (1959) suggests that the adolescent who has masturbated may later have a sense of awkwardness and body embarrassment that leads him to scan others carefully to see if his body feelings in this respect are reflected in how they see him. The menstruating woman may sensitively seek to detect if others perceive her body as being as dirty as it "feels" to her. If the masturbating adolescent knew more about the body experiences of many other masturbating adolescents or if the menstruating woman knew more about the body experiences of other menstruating women, would they not discover that their own body feelings are not grossly different from the average and would this not relieve them of the need to search the responses of others anxiously (and in rather awkward, indirect ways) for reassurance about their sense of body deviance?

The obscure, half-knowing way that the average person experiences his body probably deprives him of a lot of useful information. There are many body feelings that would help him to evaluate conditions to which he is exposed if he were clearly aware of these feelings and also believed that he could trust them. This issue often comes into focus during psychotherapeutic treatment. I have had the experience of sitting with a patient who talked at some length about an apparently pleasant, non-aggressive theme and yet noting the buildup of tension in my body. When I finally identified my body tension as a feeling of anger I was able to perceive that the patient was actually baiting me and trying to get me mad, and when the patient was confronted with his unconsciously provocative strategy he would be able to speak more openly about why he was angry at me. Young, inexperienced therapists whom I have supervised will not infrequently sit through an entire therapy session with a patient and feel discomforted by a variety of body sensations—but will treat such sensations as interfering with their job of listening to the patient instead of tuning in on them and using them as an index of what is really happening in their transactions with that patient. Therapists is training can be taught to become sensitive to their body cues and to trust them to some degree as a basis for making psychotherapeutic decisions. Of course, every person has had analogous experiences in routine life contexts. An individual may discover in the course of an apparently innocuous conversation with a friend that his body is becoming filled with unpleasant sensations. It is not atypical under such conditions to interpret such sensations as signs of possible illness or of having eaten the wrong thing or of not having had enough sleep. If the individual were more knowledgeable about his body experiences, he could, with greater accuracy, interpret what was transpiring between his friend and himself.

The truth is that our culture is dedicated to blunting the individual's skill in interpreting body experiences. Most "advanced" cultures strive for rationality and regard body arousal as likely only to mislead or to introduce irrationality into decision-making. The child is taught to make decisions "with his head." If he says he does or does not "feel like" doing something this is usually regarded as a pretty flimsy basis for acting. Action must be based on rational "reasons" rather than body feelings. Even basic body feelings like hunger or the need to defecate are typically relegated to the control of more cognitively oriented schedules, which dictate when it is proper to respond to such feelings.

Perhaps we will some day realize how much important information is cut out of the life of the average person by our present socialization practices that are so blind to, and basically suspicious of, the messages that come from the body. It would make good sense, in terms of what we already know about body perception, to provide the growing child with formal training that would help him to interpret his body more sensibly as a psychological object. We need to do so not only to affirm that it is neither irrational nor bad to tune in on the body world, but also to provide a rich vocabulary for capturing the events in that world. Aside from routine words like "anger," "fear," "tension," "headache," and "stomach ache," we need to offer terms that will capture finer shades of distinction. To illustrate, why would it not be possible for each child to learn to differentiate among the sensations in his stomach area so that he could clearly state whether he was experiencing indigestion due to eating too fast, indigestion due to eating too much, nausea expressive of a "fed-up" attitude toward the world, unpleasant stomach movements indicative of a sense of deprivation and aloneness, stomach tightness reflecting a wish to eject (vomit out) unpleasant wishes or thoughts, and so forth? Why could similar fine judgments not be learned about head sensations, heart feelings, pelvic experiences, et cetera? Such body-experience education would probably have more long-term general value in dealing well with life than so-called sex education or training in specific athletic or motor skills. It is important to emphasize that what I am suggesting differs from current faddish exhortations about "getting with" your body or enjoying nudism. I am not calling for some vague exaltation or worship of the body, but rather a practical course of training in learning to "read" your body. The term "read" applies here in almost the same sense that it does when one teaches the child to decode the information contained in words and sentences. A skeptic might ask whether people are capable of learning the fine kinds of distinctions in body state that I have proposed. I would answer that there is already scientific information available that suggests such capability. One can take the instance of obese people who, it has been found, often have difficulty in decoding stomach sensations and deciding whether they really indicate hunger. But there are now reports suggesting they can be taught to become much more accurate in this decoding process. For example, they have been assigned practical exercises that involve determining how full or empty the stomach is. In one published instance the teaching process was based on controlling the amount of fluid put into the obese individual's stomach via a tube. He had to judge repeatedly the amount of liquid inside himself. Practical training in identifying body states is also not infrequently provided to patients in psychotherapeutic treatment when it is pointed out to them that certain uncomfortable patterns of sensations they have during the therapy hour do not represent random feelings or symptoms of some minor illness but rather emotions like anger or yearnings for close contact. A new recognition of the meaning of specific body sensations may emerge as a patient learns how he hides from them defensively.

One of the consequences of people not recognizing the significance of their body sensations is that they channel the tensions from these sensations into irrelevant—even irrational—modes. A psychologist, Schachter (1967), has documented this fact in a number of ingenious experiments. He has shown that if you stir up sensations in a person's body chemically these sensations will feed into and affect concurrent emotions or attitudes. For example, if you inject adrenalin into someone and then have him watch a humorous movie, he will laugh more than a person who has not first had his body sensations augmented. Similarly, if you inject adrenalin into someone who then watches a sad movie, he will experience greater sadness than someone who watches the same movie without having received the adrenalin. The body sensations stirred up by the adrenalin apparently reinforce any concurrent emotional state. In the same way, an individual who, in real life, is flooded with body sensations that betoken some emotion but who does not recognize the emotional arousal for what it is, may find that he eventually responds in an unexpectedly exaggerated way at some other level. This may be a common source of irrationality. It highlights one of the dangers of remaining on obscure terms with one's body.

I wonder whether man's dissatisfaction with his own relationship to his body has something to do with his insatiable interest in body matters. Like any unsatisfied need it keeps churning for outlet. Because his body remains mysterious to him the average person has an urge to search out as much about the body as possible. In addition to drives like hunger and sex, there is also the need to make sense out of the mysterious body world. While a man looks at a woman for sexual reasons, he is probably also interested in the enigma of her body (as symbolic of all bodies). The permanent fascination of the nude body may, at least in part, reflect the fact that it represents a domain that is intriguing and yet relatively unknown. But aside from the stimulating, curiosity-arousing effects of the obstacles the culture places between the individual and his body, there is also a deadening impact. Because his body is disparaged and because he has had to experience it with blinders on he feels fairly alienated from it. He finds himself regarding it as somehow distant, not really his own—even foreign in its feel. This feeling has been described by the term *depersonalization,* which means that there is literally a sense of not being intimately unified with one's body—of regarding it with some detachment. Extreme forms of depersonalization have been reported by persons on LSD trips. They may suddenly feel that some parts of their bodies do not belong to them. This is particularly likely to happen with the hands. The individual looks at them and cannot shake the feeling that they are really someone else's property. An extreme form of depersonalization may be found in the psychiatric patient who becomes so involved with the notion that some part of his body is alien that he actually attempts to remove it by cutting it off. Cleveland (1956) has described a series of cases in which men have amputated their own penises, at least partially as an expression of their depersonalized attitude toward the organ. It is interesting to note that a psychiatrist, Jacobson (1959), observed feelings of depersonalization to have been prominent in Jews who were suddenly pulled out of their niche in society by the Nazis and imprisoned under circumstances that depreciated and negated their life identity. They would awaken in the middle of the night in prison with the terrorized sensation that they were not themselves— that they had become foreign things, almost detached, like inanimate objects. But aside from such extreme circumstances, there is good evidence that perfectly normal people experience depersonalization. It is not only a common feeling (Fisher, 1970), linked to the stilted way in which we require children to learn about their bodies, but also a frequent mode of reaction to stress. A sense of body "strangeness" often occurs when one feels anxious. The physiological changes associated with anxiety produce vivid body sensations that are so different from one's usual body state that they may be disturbingly intense and lead to defensive reactions like "that isn't me" or "my body doesn't feel like that." As already mentioned, feelings of body strangeness are particularly likely to be localized in the hands; it is not uncommon to try to counteract them by rubbing the hands together or touching other objects. There is increasing evidence that people rub, touch, or finger parts of their bodies as a way of coping with alien feelings emanating from them. Hollender (1970) has even described women who promiscuously seek sexual intercourse, not because they particularly enjoy intercourse, but rather as a means of getting someone to hold and caress their bodies (which are experienced in an unpleasantly depersonalized fashion).

The extreme response to feelings of depersonalization encountered in some psychiatric patients, as just mentioned, is probably paralleled in other extreme forms of acting-out involving the body. We know that some of the appeal of alcohol and other drugs resides in the intense body experiences they produce. Bodies that feel dead and alienated may be brought to a novel state. Sensations of excitement, changes in apparent size, dizziness, warmth and cold, and others of an even more florid character may be stirred up. The "far away" body can suddenly and dramatically feel closer and more personalized.

Body depersonalization is actually encouraged by many of our current customs and fads. The woman who is repeatedly confronted by clothing style changes that she is supposed to adopt, whether or not they are compatible to her own feelings about her body, comes to perceive her body as not terribly different from a department store mannequin. Her body is simply one more standardized frame and, as such, seems perhaps to belong more to the culture than to herself. The force of this body standardization is highlighted if you consider that it applies not only to a woman's outer clothing, but also her underwear, her hair style, the cosmetics she applies to her face, fingers, and toes, the respectable limits of the kind of aroma she can emit, and even the angle of tilt of her breasts. In some ways, the body standardization for men is even more extreme.

There are a lot of strategies that ordinary people use to fight body depersonalization. They smoke, eat spicy foods, take sauna baths, and seek out as much sexual stimulation as possible. They also drive at body-wrenching speed, take dizzy whirls and stand in front of distorting mirrors in amusement parks, empathically watch people do strange things with their bodies in the circus, parachute out of airplanes, engage in head-standing Yoga exercises, and soak up sun to the point of skin damage. Further, they wear masks, get themselves tattooed, try plastic surgery, and don painfully tight appliances. Even further, they masturbate, become addicted to rhythmic tic-like body movements with plenty of kinesthetic energy, and bombard themselves with loud stimuli (like amplified stereo music) that come close to stirring pain in receptors.

In other words, to employ one's body actively or forcefully is to combat depersonalization. But so many factors are arrayed against such activity, not the least of which are forces like television and the whole game of becoming educated. A person who sits for hours in front of the TV set, rarely moving his body and acting primarily as a one-channel passive receptor, is more than metaphorically treating his body as a passive (and somewhat alien) object. Similarly, a successful career as a student calls for endless hours of sitting (with body almost immovable) while absorbing information from books. The body is largely superfluous to the whole scholastic enterprise. An interesting insight into the relationship that exists between scholastic devotion and body attitudes has come from the work of Kagan and Moss (1962). They were in a position to follow the lives of a number of persons from birth to late adolescence. They found that boys who went on to become good students and invested in intellectuality were typically afraid of the body world in their younger years. Their parents instilled in them anxiety about potential body damage, and their teachers noted that they avoided activities in which there was the possibility of getting hurt. In other words, intellectuality and body security were found to be in opposition in boys. One could interpret the intellectuality as a compensation. This was not true for girls. More will be said about such sex differences in a later chapter.

Depersonalization is magnified in situations where a person feels that he is surrendering his body to another person or power greater than himself. It is fear of such surrender that seems to inhibit many persons from seeking medical consultation when they first discover some malfunction in their bodies. The average person is quite irrational in the way he conducts himself when he becomes aware of a body symptom. He delays and delays, putting off seeking the services of a physician. This is true, by the way, even of physicians themselves and of other well-educated persons who have the technical knowledge to be aware that they are behaving recklessly. To go for medical consultation in our culture signifies giving up an important chunk of your body autonomy. You submit your body to probing and investigation that could eventuate in catastrophic information about the state of your health and the need for even more radical surrender of body autonomy, such as would be required if one had to submit to surgery or go to the hospital for some form of treatment. There is a striking paradox in what happens to the body from a psychological perspective when someone becomes a patient in a hospital. On the one hand, it suddenly becomes possible to focus intense interest on your own body and to do so in an acceptable way; but on the other hand, you are told in numerous ways that your body no longer is your own. It belongs to the hospital establishment in which you have taken up residence. It becomes public property, subject to the probing and care that issue from the special logic of medical and nursing principles. The disposition of one's body does, for all practical purposes, leave the realm of personal decision and becomes a function of a system. This is experienced by the average individual as depersonalization of his body. It has been documented that other institutions (for example, prisons) can have a similar depersonalizing impact. In fact, depersonalization of the body is deliberately applied by some organizations (for example, the military's use of hair-cutting and imposition of a uniform that masks body individuality) to maintain control over its members. This obviously implies that body depersonalization renders one more malleable and susceptible to domination.

The persistent enigma of a man's body takes on added consequence if you consider that his body feelings are, from moment to moment, mixing into his impressions of the world, whether he wants them to or not. When body sensations are of either the very pleasant or the very unpleasant variety their impact upon other perceptions is obvious. That is, if your body is in pain or if, at the obvious extreme, you feel awfully good because you have just eaten a good meal, you will be very aware of how such sensations are coloring your overall perceptions. But there are also numerous, less obvious ways in which they form a grid or system of coordinates upon which life impressions are traced. I have conducted a number of experiments in which I have shown that body attitudes, even those of which the individual may be unaware consciously himself, may influence his responses to unstructured stimuli like ink blots. If his body feels open, vulnerable, and unprotected, he will be inclined, in his imaginative interpretations of Rorschach ink blots, to conjure up images that reek of vulnerability (for example, "wounded man," "bullet piercing flesh"). If his body feels safe and protected he is more likely to produce "well-protected" images like "fort," "man in armor," "in a cave with rocky walls," "man inside of a church." Relatedly, everyone has had the experience of looking at a landscape one time and finding it intrusively threatening and then on another occasion being impressed by its peaceful, protective qualities. I am suggesting that the difference might very well have mirrored contrasting body "moods" or attitudes. One group of investigators (Wapner and Werner, 1965) reported that if you look at some object and are aware that it has a special significance to your body it will seem to have different qualities than if you do not assign it such a special role. For example, it will appear in the first instance to be closer to you in space than it does in the second instance. Still another investigator reported that people tell different kinds of imaginative stories when they are lying down and when they are sitting up. One could say that simply altering the position of a person's body in space can influence the way in which he uses his imagination. Indeed, the procedure of placing the patient in a reclining position on a couch that is used by most psychoanalysts is based, to some extent, on the notion that the process of free association is easier in a reclining than in an upright posture. There are plenty of instances in everyday life in which physiognomic interpretations issue from complex body feelings. The adolescent, whose body necessarily feels radically altered, may see the whole world as unstable and imminently ready for radical alteration. A woman who has been told in various ways that her body is ugly and who has accepted this idea may not be able to grasp the existence of beauty elsewhere. The man who for his own reasons regards his body, or some part of it, as smaller than it should be may be particularly vulnerable to a sense of intimidation when he walks into a large building or is in the presence of an impressive machine. Apropos of this matter of the interaction between sense of body size and the experience of spatial size "out there," a man whom I was treating psychotherapeutically showed the first sign of serious psychological disturbance in the form of a feeling that doorways were too narrow for his body to pass through. But consider some further examples of how body attitudes may find expression in conclusions about the world. The individual who feels that his body is full of emotion, that it is a container packed with feelings under high pressure, may project this feeling and see other objects as pumped up with the same kind of pressure. He may mistakenly see other persons as barely able to contain their emotions or perceive even inanimate things as suffused with unexpected intensity. They may seem more vivid or less controlled than usual. It is such an orientation that might have contributed to one psychiatric patient's remarking that, "The whole world looks like it's ready to blow up." Finally, consider the example of the person who experiences his own body as so overcontrolled and confining (because of the overstrict demands by his parents for control of his body functions) that he responds to any restricted space as if it were explosively smothering him. A psychiatric patient of mine, for example, would become extremely perturbed whenever he had to spend much time in a small room or confined area. The walls of a room seemed to press in on him in the same way that the restricting walls of his own body were experienced.

These examples of how body attitudes infiltrate the "feel" of the world have been cited as a way of leading into a discussion of the consequences of our growing up with bodies that we experience as only half known and somewhat disreputable.

I would conjecture that one large consequence is that we attribute to what is "out there" some of the same "half-known" qualities. The world seems to mirror back to us that it is a confusing place—full of mysterious attributes that smack of potential badness. We expect, in a fashion somewhat analogous to our feelings about our bodies, that things out there cannot be clearly grasped or understood. In other words, I am suggesting that the doubt and the almost uncanny mystery that halo many of our images of external reality directly reflect how we feel about our corporeal base of operations. Relatedly, feelings of being "in the dark" and unable to impose order on events may reflect analogous sensations about the nature of one's body. Much has been made of the fact that man in every part of the world has responded to the phenomena of nature by personifying them. He has consistently tied natural events to agents that he pictures to be human in form. But always the agents are assigned esoteric Godlike or monster-like qualities. They are mysterious and strange. Is this brand of personification a transposition of the "unknown body"? Interestingly, many of the distortions assigned to the Movers of Nature resemble those often encountered in the individual's perception of his own body. The portrayal of such figures as unusually large or small, possessed of unique combinations of masculine and feminine traits, or having extra or too few parts duplicates similar distortions that are common in the body-image fantasies of most people at some phase of their development.

The myths of every culture are saturated with tales of the strange things that can happen to the human body. There seems to be no limit to the potential for bizarre transformation ascribed to the body. The world is seen as full of byways in which mutilating forces lie in wait. Our uncertainties about the properties of our flesh are dramatic and widespread. According to older myths, your body can be turned to stone, transformed into that of an animal or even some form of vegetation, changed to the opposite sex, reshaped into a murderous monster, given an evil immortality, and so forth. There are also modern myths that convey a similar message. In more up-to-date terms, you are faced with the possibility of being born a monster as the result of your mother having been exposed to radiation, experiencing bizarre alterations in body as the result of ingesting LSD, finding a vital part of yourself surgically transplanted, losing unbelievable chunks of your body in the course of surgery for cancer, being able to survive only by having your body hooked up to some gadget like an iron lung or a kidney machine, or being turned into a mechanical robot in the course of some futuristic science fiction yarn.

We know so little about our mysterious bodies and yet they confront us everywhere.

The intent of this chapter has been to orient the reader to the primary difficulties that tax him as he tries to make rational sense of his body. His confusion about his body reflects a culture-wide irrationality about body phenomena. This irrationality stems not only from the distorted symbolic meanings assigned to the body and the anxious need to avoid directly contemplating its vulnerability, but also from its continually changing qualities. The first step in arriving at a generally more sensible style of body perception is to analyze our sources of confusion. Each individual will then be in a better position to trace out the special confusions that apply to him. This review of our problems in adapting to our own bodies is also intended to lay the groundwork for understanding the complex body-image defenses that will be described in the chapters that follow.

CHAPTER TWO

Defense of the border

The story of the Three Little Pigs dramatizes a task that we all face. After many trials and tribulations, the swine hero of that story finds a way of establishing a home base where he can be reasonably well protected against intrusion by hostile outsiders like hungry wolves. His brick house proves to be a safe fortress. His success was a result of building his house of materials strong enough to stand up to tough onslaught. Similarly, each person in the world has to learn how to feel secure in that most fundamental home base of all, his body. He has to develop confidence that the walls of his body can adequately shield him from all of the potentially bad things "out there." Without such confidence, he will live frightened, expecting the wolf to break in at any moment. There is little that a person can do about the literal strength of the materials that constitute his body. Rather, his struggle to establish body security takes place at a more psychological level. There is good research evidence (Fisher, 1970) that he learns, in the course of growing up, to have a certain amount of trust in the protective power of the flesh that girds the periphery of his body. What we have found is that some people clearly visualize their bodies as possessing a boundary, or border, that separates them from what is out there and is capable of withstanding alien things that might try to intrude upon them. But there are others who have trouble perceiving their bodies as separate or possessed of a defensible border.[1] They feel open and vulnerable. The difference between the person with clearly defined body boundaries and the person who feels only vaguely "set off" can be compared to the contrast between a knight who goes into battle with his shiny armor fastened in place and someone playing at knighthood who wears fake armor made of cardboard.

This chapter will lead the reader through an analysis of how he builds up a sense of possessing an individualized body, one that belongs to himself. It will point out the forces that enhance and disrupt body-boundary safety and describe the maneuvers that people use to protect their body borders. Suggestions will be made about possible ways to enhance border security.

If you ask the average person about his body boundary, you will get only a puzzled look. While he knows that all structures have walls and defining limits, he has probably never applied this idea to his own body. If pressed, he will admit, "Of course, there are boundaries to my body. My body is enclosed by skin and that skin marks the edge of me." But he is rarely aware that he has learned basic attitudes about that "edge of me" and whether it is substantial and defensible. To make a large-scale comparison, nations also have boundaries and differ in how secure they feel about them: no one in the United States worries about the vulnerability of the borders with Canada, but the Czechs were frantic in their feeling of vulnerability about their border with Germany. In any case, the average person does not become aware of his sense of possessing a psychologically defined body boundary and of its potent functions until something happens to him that seriously disturbs these functions. There are people afflicted with severe brain damage who lose the ability to distinguish whether an event is occurring on the surface of the body or somewhere "out there." If you ask such a person to close his eyes and to designate the place where you touch his skin, he may point to a spot completely beyond his body. He literally can not locate his body limits. Precipitous and dramatic loss of boundary can be found, too, in some schizophrenic individuals. One disturbed woman (Schilder, 1935) experienced anything that happened in her vicinity as though it were somehow getting into her body.

[1] Quantitative methods for measuring a person's feeling about the substantiality of his body boundary have been devised that are based on the nature of responses given to ink blots (Fisher and Cleveland, 1968).

For example, if a car passed her on the street she felt as if it were literally running over the organs inside her body. There are accounts in the psychiatric literature of psychotics who cannot tell whether a hallucinated voice is coming from within their own bodies or from a more distant source. They are strangely confused about what is inside and what is outside. In these gross instances one can detect the role of the boundary because it is not doing the taken-for-granted things it usually does.

Normal persons can also become acutely aware of the role of the body boundary when they lose it under extraordinary circumstances. A good example is provided by Lilly, a psychiatrist, who studied the effects of submerging himself in a tank of water whose temperature was the same as his body. He floated inside this tank with all light and sound excluded. It was like being in the womb of a mammoth creature. Lilly discovered that after a while he could not distinguish where his body left off and the water began; he felt merged and indistinguishable from all that surrounded him. His sense of self was radically dissipated. Similar experiences have been reported by some persons who have taken LSD. They begin to feel that they are "opened up," oceanically fused with the world. What happens "out there" and "in here" seem to be one. The LSD may also excite the sensation that one's body is soft or non-cohesive; parts may feel as if they are detached.

All living matter is characterized by cell membranes and other delineating mechanisms that guard against the wrong kind of input. People expend enormous energy in setting up defensive boundaries. They erect buildings, forts, and shelters, and when nothing else is available burrow into the ground or seek refuge in a cave. They also cover their bodies with protective and concealing clothing, and—more symbolically—adorn themselves with tattoos, cosmetics, paints, decorations, and an unending variety of embellishing appliances. They even throw up screens between themselves and others that are based on the effects of scents (perfumes or garlic, for example) upon olfactory sensibilities. Research findings suggest that the greater a person's uncertainty about the protection provided by his own body border the more he will seek compensatory ways of reaffirming that border. One investigator (Compton, 1964) found that schizophrenic women tried to reassure themselves about their borders by wearing loud checked clothing. Another (Kernaleguen, 1968) found that those college women who are most insecure about their boundaries are likely to take the lead in wearing the newest clothing fashions—which would certainly make them among the most visible sartorially. In other words, when an individual doubts his boundaries he may try to reinforce them by making them more visually vivid through the use of attention-getting clothing. I wonder whether uniforms may not be often similarly employed. The soldier with his helmet and decorated chest and the motorcycle policeman with his leather gloves and boots may gain a good measure of security from their official cocoons. One psychologist (Popplestone, 1963) has compared putting on a uniform to providing yourself with a protective exoskeleton similar to that possessed by lobsters and turtles. It might also be compared to being draped with a security blanket. While there is as yet no scientific evidence available on this point, I would speculate that being inside the gleaming, metal capsule of a highspeed car also provides great backup for weak body boundaries. To be embedded in a sports car whizzing along so fast that no one can gain access to it probably offers massive reassurance about being bodily separate from others.

I have observed in my research with schizophrenic women that they may use self-touching and self-caressing as a means of telling themselves that the "edge of me" is there and intact. Everyone engages in frequent self-touching and has no doubt had the experience in a stressful situation of finding that the feel of his own hands on his skin is comforting and reassuring. The boundary-reassuring value of friendly touching probably motivates people to do a lot of things to their own bodies. They have invented a thousand rituals to provide awareness of their borders. They rub themselves with lotions and oils, apply hot and cold to their surfaces, and massage their muscles. They put on tight garments that articulate large body segments. One of the rewards that may drive people to expose themselves mercilessly to the sun may be the boundary-reinforcing effect of feeling the sun's rays over a wide body area (not to mention the visual reinforcement of seeing the skin darkened and more vivid because of its changed appearance). Friendly touching comes, too, from sexual contact. As mentioned earlier, Hollender (1970) has found that some women value intercourse primarily for the cuddling and skin contact it provides. With reference to sexual stimulation, even some of the so-called perversions that involve practices like flagellation may, in a paradoxical way, be valued for the heightened awareness they bring to the outer layers of the body—beating the skin highlights it dramatically. Similarly, there are psychotics who have verbalized the idea that they have cut themselves or banged some body part against the wall because they wanted to regain a clear picture of the dimensionality of their bodies, which had become vague and "deadened."

The long-term appeal to us of certain forms and symbols may derive from the fact that they indirectly bolster our boundaries. The image of the clown with his painted face and his exaggerated garb certainly emphasizes the body façade and the importance of the body surface. The performer with his flamboyant mask who appears on the stage in so many cultures conveys a similar message. The beautiful actress wrapped in a gorgeous costume is calling attention to the value and power of the body surface. Symbols that depict space enclosed by a protective periphery may offer a reassuring analogy of our body space. Pictures that incorporate images like the ship, the impregnable castle, the trophy cup, the enclosed body of water, and the peaceful valley surrounded by hills communicate a belief in the dependability of that which encloses. A recurrent theme in American folklore is that of the pioneer under attack who manages to survive and even gain victory by forming a defensive circle with his covered wagons and fighting from behind this almost magical barrier. In more up-to-date form this theme appears again and again in fantasies of being an invulnerable Superman or an astronaut who braves dangerous space in the technologically perfected cocoon of his space craft. More peacefully, it surfaces in the idyllic fantasy of being cast away on a distant lush tropical island. One psychiatrist has said that in the course of observing the ceramic shapes constructed by schizophrenics she was struck by the fact that their improvement was often heralded by the increasingly concave form of their constructions. That is, they began to create forms that were hollow and protected by bounding walls. This was interpreted by the psychiatrist as a return of the feeling that the patient possessed a body with real protective boundaries. The sense of being open and vulnerable was replaced by a feeling of once again having a defensible border—a place within which to take a stand in the world.

The amount of distance that we place between ourselves and others may well announce how secure our borders feel. There is some objective evidence (Fisher, 1970) that those who have "shaky" boundaries are inclined to keep their distance. If you are not too close to others there is less chance that they can launch a successful intrusion against you. It is the person with a sense of assurance about his borders who feels more at ease in groups and who takes the initiative in being friendly and receptive. The isolate, standing off at the edge of the party, probably fears what closeness may bring. His anxiety about being intruded upon may variously take such forms as concern about being ridiculed, unpleasant sensitivity to the expression of strong emotion by anyone else, or even a literal dread of being physically attacked. An extreme clinical manifestation of closeness dread is provided by the male patient in a "homosexual panic state" who is terrified by the fantasy that some man will violate him by thrusting his penis into his rectum. Any hint of closeness to another man means primarily that he will be exposed to an alien force that might destructively gain entrance to his insides. There are whole nations and subcultures that have been terribly afraid of contact with others and have dreaded the penetration that might be initiated by "Outsiders." The earlier defensive isolation of the Japanese represents a good example. The careful self-sealing-off of certain monastic religious orders offers another kind of example. One wonders whether such fear of outside contact does not have its origin in a basic distrust of the integrity of one's own body. This is a question that can still be profitably investigated.

Some people find that strong emotion helps them to locate their boundaries more accurately. The feel of their body arousal when they are emotionally stirred up gives them a greater sense of tissue solidity. Their excitement makes their bodies seem more real; this applies also to the tissue that girds the body periphery. Two investigators (Kaufman and Heims, 1958) have described interestingly how certain delinquent adolescents may seek experiences in which they can be hostile and aggressive because the very act of feeling angry has self-delineating effects. They noted that many of these aggressive-acting adolescents felt "opened up" and vulnerable and uncertain of their personal limits unless they could get angry. The experience of anger permitted them to define their individuality. One is reminded of the typical Camus character who feels dead and without identity and only glimpses himself as a bounded entity when he explodes into an act of violence. We know little about the self-validating impact of being emotionally aroused, but I would conjecture that eating, with its associated body sensations, may have important self-defining significance for many. Sexual arousal, elation, and even certain brands of anxiety may function similarly for others. The individual who has to keep moving, who has to maintain himself in a super-busy, charged-up state may, in the final analysis, be primarily dedicated to asserting that his body is an activated and therefore palpably separate object.

When we are placed in situations where we lose the support of our auxiliary boundary defenses, we become more concerned about the solidity of our own body periphery. In an old Nick Carter magazine that I once read the hero captured a criminal and decided that the best way to extract some important information from him was to make him remove his clothes. By so doing, he expected that the criminal would feel vulnerable and defenseless and so be more easily scared into "singing." Needless to say, his strategy worked perfectly. We recently carried out an experiment in our psychology laboratory that tangentially tested some elements of Nick Carter's assumption. In the course of a study of sexual responsiveness in women we came to wonder whether the nudity that frequently accompanies sexual intercourse is threatening and perhaps plays a role in the sexual response difficulties of some women (Fisher, 1973). That is, if a woman's clothing provides some reinforcement for her borders and helps to decrease feelings of vulnerability, what happens when she is left with only her skin as a covering? We measured boundary feelings both before and after a number of women removed their clothing (in preparation for a physiological procedure in which they had only a sheet loosely draped around them) and found that the greater a woman's difficulty in attaining orgasm the greater was her sense of boundary loss when her clothes were removed. It is not a big jump to the conclusion that one of the factors that may interfere with a woman reaching orgasm is the sense of disturbing vulnerability linked with the removal of her "second skin."

There are people who react with anxiety as soon as they leave the protective walls of their homes. In some instances this anxiety is so overwhelming that the individual cannot give up the shelter of the home walls at all or at best only briefly. Clinically, this is referred to as agoraphobia. Persons with this syndrome are scared out of their wits when they find themselves out in the open. They expect some terrible thing to happen that threatens their very existence. The language they use in describing their anxiety indicates a feeling of being open to some unnamed catastrophic invasion. While there is no scientific evidence on this point, it is my hypothesis that they lack any sense of body-boundary integrity. The walls of the house substitute for their body walls, so going out into the open is equivalent to an old Apache torture in which the victim is flayed alive. There are people who get a bit scared when they cannot wear a favorite ring or decoration that symbolically gives strength to the body surface. Others do not feel right until they have squeezed into girdles or put on wrist watches or pulled on boots. I have talked with several disturbed adolescents who insisted on wearing heavy leather jackets at all times, even on hot days, because they felt upset unless embraced by their reassuring synthetic cauls. Interestingly, I have also heard a very obese man say that he could not stand to lose weight because he regarded his layers of fat as a protective armoring wrapped around his torso. When he lost weight he felt like a man who was forced to remove his flak jacket just before coming under fire.

A number of years ago one of the favorite methods that was used to quiet a disturbed schizophrenic was to wrap him tightly in a wet sheet. He was encased in what amounted to a moist bag that kept him immobile. Some have considered the procedure to be inhumane; others who observed it were impressed by the relief it brought to highly disturbed, "out-of-control" psychotics. They attributed its success to the fact that it provided the patient with a substitute mode of restraint for that ordinarily supplied by the inhibiting power of his own musculature. In other words, it provided a substitute body wall. We have all immersed ourselves in hot tubs at some time of crisis and found the wrap-around warm skin contact to be calming and reassuring. A parent sometimes intuitively does an analogous thing when he responds to a child throwing a wild tantrum by holding him tightly against his body. He substitutes his own body to give the child the restraining enclosure he cannot muster by himself.

The walls of our shelters and buildings represent one of the major ways in which we literally provide reinforcement for our body boundaries. If we studied the matter, we might find a relationship between how a person feels about his boundaries and the kind of house in which he chooses to live. Does the person with vague borders avoid living in a house whose walls are extensively comprised of glass and therefore not substantially protective? Does the amount of open space in a house relate to whether the owner needs to feel protectively nestled by enclosing walls? We know absolutely nothing at this point about such phenomena, but we do have some evidence that the space in which we dwell affects body feelings. One investigator (Fisher, 1970) asked college students to spend some time in a miniature room in which even the furniture had been reduced to comparable scale. He found that this experience did alter their perception of their body sizes. By direct analogy, I would expect people who occupy buildings of grandiose size to perceive their bodies as having size properties different from those who inhabit some of the stunted, squeezed-in structures that can be seen everywhere.

In a purely speculative way, I have asked myself to identify the body-image implications of the architectural features most character-istic of Western culture. Although not being an architect I am not really qualified to answer this question, I have singled out one obvious development in Western architecture as a starting point for thought. The image of the skyscraper—simple, streamlined, sheathed in light or transparent materials—is often equated with what is unique about our modern architectural perspective. One of my major impressions of such structures is that while they seek to dramatize their equation with the powerful, technologically perfect machine, they evoke sensa-tions of vulnerability in their inhabitants. Someone living in a glass-walled skyscraper cannot but perceive the wondrous "machine" that it is. In many ways, it is comparable to a great space vehicle ready for a journey. Certainly it symbolizes the power of technical con-struction. It soars off the ground, effortlessly defies gravity, and can withstand enormous stresses despite the apparent fragility of its walls. But at the same time that this message of superb machine-like power is conveyed, the inhabitant is also aware that he is suspended high up in space and enclosed by materials that seem weak for their intended function. When you are way up there your body gives you all kinds of signals about the strangeness of your position. The apparatus in your nervous system concerned with balance gets tuned up to a fine, touchy state. In other words, the skyscraper expects you to accept on faith that a powerful machine can be trusted. But visually and kines-thetically it is experienced as potentially dangerous and little is done, in terms of the outer appearance of the structure, to allay anxiety. The individual is expected to ignore the protests of his body about its unique suspension in space and to focus instead on the reassurances he gets from the ideas in his head about the efficiency of machine-like structures. One could say that the skyscraper throws back on the in-dividual's body the task of maintaining a sense of being adequately protected. He finds little in the boundaries of the skyscraper to bolster his security, but rather has to fall back on his own boundary resources. It might be interesting to analyze other aspects of modern architecture to determine if they give the same ambivalent message about providing protective shelter to the inner dweller.

The entire experience of dwelling in the city, as such, may help people to feel more secure about their boundaries. The city is a cir-cumscribed region of land and in previous days even had solid-looking walls reinforcing its perimeter. It is a place full of people in which nature has been conquered and reduced to the regulated order of water pipes, paved streets, square corners, and orderly rows of houses that can obviously stand up to any display of the weather. Passage through the city takes place on well-defined streets that are walled in by the houses lining each side. There is guaranteed security against uncontrolled natural events. Even the control of fellow human inhabitants is promised by elaborate systems of signs and lights and also by time and duty definitions that tell people when and where they can go. It is because of the promise of the city as a place where the individual's boundaries will not be intruded upon that so much rage is generated by "crime on the street" involving assault on, and in some instances rape of, the body. The idea that the city is not safe means that man's most carefully regulated "stake-out" in the world has failed in its mission. If the city system can be breached, is your own body next?

There are certain situations or demands that are especially likely to churn up anxiety about losing one's boundaries. This is apt to happen when there is a literal threat to the integrity of the body. If a person finds that he is going to be exposed to things that can penetrate his molecular structure he gets anxious about his boundary holding up. The person who is about to have a hypodermic needle plunged into his body by a physician is having some of the same thoughts as a general who sees on his map that an enemy spearhead has breached his defense line at one point. Obviously, procedures like surgery raise even more dramatic doubts. Whenever anything mechanical is inserted into the body it causes boundary disturbance, no matter how reassuring the conditions under which it is done. Among physicians it is well known how difficult it is to persuade people to undergo an examination such as is involved when a proctoscope is inserted into the rectum. Cancer agencies that have urged people to seek routine rectal examinations have been unsuccessful in their efforts. Indeed, some people exhibit rather extreme forms of anxiety during rectal examinations, ranging from near panic to gross vascular spasms. Procedures involving almost any body opening, with its clear channel through the boundary into the body interior, seem to be alarming. The dread of the dentist who will poke his instruments into your mouth is an obvious example. A psychologist (Lane, 1966) who studied the dreams of persons who were about to undergo surgery found that they were painfully focused on images portraying the body as under mutilating attack. Children who are hospital patients become preoccupied with fantasies of body damage (Schneider, 1960). The fear of being hurt and penetrated by anyone who approaches one's body with a sharp instrument may become so intense that it even prevents going to a barber. One schizophrenic man initially evidenced his breakdown in a dread of going to the barbershop. He had all kinds of wild fantasies about how the barber might mutilate him.

There are forces in the world that may be working to decrease the general level of boundary security. I will not belabor the obvious ones. Anyone who gets around knows that it is scary to have atomic bombs poised for action that can blow your body to smithereens. You are bound to have just a bit less assurance about the tensile strength of your peripheral tissue. There are a lot of other obvious things that can make you doubt your ability to stand up to intrusion: the polluted air that introduces harmful material into your body interior; the crowding that puts you closer, on a chronic basis, to the bodies of strangers whose potential for aggression is unknown; and the exposure to giant machine fabrications (whether they be buildings or devices) that are so manifoldly more powerful than the human frame that they could obviously go through you like jelly. These are some of the obvious intrusive forces. But there are also more subtle ones that may be just as incisive. I would single out the incessant input of the television screen as being of special import. The average child grows up in our culture with the television machine transplanted into his visual system. There are few visual sources in his world that he focuses on so energetically and devotedly. As McLuhan pointed out, the TV set becomes an extension of one's own nervous system. I am literally suggesting that the minute-to-minute, day-by-day, month-by-month, year-by-year process of relating to the TV screen finally results in it becoming psychologically part of the individual's self-realm. It becomes an auxiliary to his body in the same way that a habitually worn pair of glasses or piece of jewelry does. When he is separated from it he becomes uncomfortable, as if he were kept from making contact with his favorite teddy bear. The intense ego closeness of the TV screen is evidenced by the fact that many schizophrenic persons now develop elaborate delusional systems either about television itself (for example, that it is spying on them) or about the figures that are exhibited on it. I am speculating that the person who grows up vis-à-vis the TV machine begins to feel that it is a permanent auxiliary to his sensory apparatus. It is as if he has another widely scanning set of eyes. But even further, he finds that the input from these eyes exceeds in total drama, authority, and hoopla what he gets from his own local visual inspection of the world. This terribly important auxiliary to his own visual apparatus becomes a major source of input. After a while he feels that he is being subjected to an input process over which he really has little control. He is so attached to the TV machine, so exposed to it, and so inexorably sold by repetition on the validity of what it reveals to him that he gets the sensation that it represents a rent in his boundary. It keeps pouring material into him whether he wants this to happen or not. I would argue that feeling opened up to such input makes the average person feel that he has lost some control over his boundaries.

Another subtle factor that wears away boundary integrity is the pervasive faith in the value of drugs and related magic potions. In ways that are too tricky to trace the average person is given the message that "out there" in the world are stocks of substances that, if ingested in the proper dosage, will cure him of disease, maintain the proper chemical balance inside his body, relieve him of headache, and even make him happy. He is led to feel that his body is incomplete without the potential for access to drugs. This means that the idea is instilled that there is no such thing as an independent body. It is as if some essential element of your body existed elsewhere and you knew that sooner or later you would have to bring it into your body in order to keep going. I would suggest that this sense of being bodily incomplete without union with the right drug leaves another kind of rent in the body boundary. The individual feels some lack in his own delineation because, in a sense, he has to keep an aperture open for attachment to the drug umbilicus when it becomes necessary.

I think a similar effect may be ascribed to the intensified vision that we all have before us of the later years of life as a battle between the pathology of aging and the techniques developed by science for prolonging survival. There is a new image of old age. It is not simply the final phase before you die; rather it has become a time when your own body finally fails in its efforts at independent survival and it becomes necessary to put it in tandem with some gadget that will pump in the necessary compensatory currents or juices. There is an inevitable time when your body will be hooked to something else and you will be terribly dependent on that something else. The standard concept now circulating in our culture is that a man's body is no longer a fairly independent entity. People are resigned to the idea that the body must ultimately receive and incorporate an alien appliance. Note what one psychiatrist has remarked about this matter: "The 'Prosthetic Man' is now a reality of modern technology. Karel Capek's *robot*, Mary Shelley's Frankenstein, and E. T. A. Hoffman's Olympia have their present-day counterparts in such patients as those with artificial heart valves, cardiac pacemakers, and artificial kidneys" (Abram, 1970, p. 475). Incidentally, while people are glad to have new ways of surviving, the underlying feeling about being attached to life-saving gadgets is one of despair. Enough time has passed so that a lot of information has accumulated about people who need to be partially mechanized. For example, a good deal is known about the feelings and attitudes of those who have lost kidney function and survive through hemodialysis. They are chronically depressed and withdraw into narrowed perspectives. They really have to wear psychological blinders and rarely get charged up about anything. There is evidence that their suicide rate is extremely high. It is also pertinent that even those persons who have had flesh-and-blood hearts transplanted into them manifest as yet unexplained difficulties in psychological adjustment, not infrequently becoming psychotic.

Paradoxically, some people are strangely attracted to boundary loss. They seek the means to divest themselves of their sense of differentiation and to merge with all that surrounds them. They are scared by the experience and yet drawn to it. This is certainly true of many persons who take LSD. With some alarm, but even more curiosity, they watch their borders fade and the distance between themselves and other objects shrink to zero. There is a unique thrill, a gamble with basic identity. It is a way not only of shedding what may be an unpleasant concept of self but also of losing all awareness of responsibility. Perhaps, too, it is for some a way of intimately contacting a world from which they have felt excluded. The person who has long stood inside his own body and felt that he could not touch others may be willing to try a new dramatic way of demolishing the barriers that keep him in. One psychoanalyst (Peto, 1959) has described instances in which psychiatric patients he was treating would, as part of their attempts to establish an intimate relationship with him, conjure up fantasies in which their flesh melted and flowed and moulded itself on to him. Note his observations of one patient (p. 3):

> Then she (patient) hallucinated the following: a gradual shrinking of her body, turning into a baby and being cuddled and held with infinite care by the analyst. In the hallucination the analyst's whole body softened up, gradually lost shape and became jelly-like or even liquid. Then that patient's minute body, which had softened up to the same extent, penetrated the analyst's body or merged with it.
>
> . . . she (patient) began to feel a gradual enlargement of her limbs and her vulva. They were hers and yet they were not. . . . They continued growing and engulfed the analyst and the whole room.

It may be that all intimacy, even when it is purely verbal, retains its original sense of involving body closeness. The idea of intimacy is actually best conveyed by the image of two bodies pressed closely together. To relate to another person intimately is to open oneself and to permit a closeness of approach rarely allowed to anyone. Fantasies of merging (as in sexual intercourse) may be prominent. Intimacy means, then, a giving up *to some degree* of the differentiation between one's own body and that of another. Obviously, we are talking about boundary loss. I recall that in one exploratory (unpublished) study we found that persons who were engaged to marry were lower in boundary definiteness than non-engaged (and unmarried) persons. Can it be that the decision to unite in marriage, with the customary accompanying massive increase in body intimacy, results in some loss of self-delineation at that time? We badly need research to clarify this matter.

Another popular way of savoring boundary loss is to submerge yourself in a flow of stimulation. This frequently occurs in the play of adolescents who expose themselves to music of piercing intensity at the same time that they are visually bombarded by strobe lights and other dramatic flashings. They strive to "escape from self," to arrive at a state where they cannot clearly distinguish themselves from their jumping, vibrating contexts. They seek to merge with it all. In view of the actual finding that adolescence itself is a time when there is an unusual amount of uncertainty about personal boundaries, it is interesting that so many adolescents experiment with boundary loss. One would think that an individual who is unclear about his boundaries would refrain from exposing himself to conditions that are boundary disruptive. But it may be that the uncertain adolescent experiments in order to master his uncertainty. By exposing himself to a boundary-disruptive situation that is fairly mild and that he can really leave whenever he wants to do so and proving to himself that he can adapt to and even enjoy it he builds up confidence in himself as an independent entity. Experimenting with loss of boundaries also amounts to sampling what it feels like to slough off one's usual controls and to let whatever is inside pour out freely. It is for this reason, too, that the adolescent, who is so often caught up in the temptation to jettison the accepted values and restraints, may find boundary dissolution so tempting. I would suggest that the boundary provides security not only because it seems to guard against attack from "out there" but also because it holds in "stuff" that should not get out. Just as having a functional anal sphincter provides security against non-scheduled extrusion of a substance from "inside," which would be terribly embarrassing, the feeling of having a well-delineated boundary offers reassurance that bad fantasies and wishes and emotions will not "break out" into public view. It has been found in several instances (Fisher, 1970) that those who have poor control over their impulses and who are inclined to rash acting-out are typified by a feeling that their boundaries are fragile. They feel that they lack the ability to keep confined what is generated within themselves, so, as soon as the inner pressure of emotions begins to accumulate they get sensations of "bursting" and "blowing up."

We are only beginning to glimpse the consequences of how people experience their body borders. There have been quite a number of scattered observations that implicate this experience in what appear to be widely separated areas of behavior. One study (Fisher, 1972) indicated that the more defensible a woman considers her boundaries the greater the number of intercourse positions she and her husband make use of each month. In another research report we find that the more definite a girl's boundaries the less likely she is to develop certain kinds of menstrual difficulties when she leaves home to attend college (Fisher and Osofsky, 1967). Even further, we are told (Cassell and Hemingway, 1970) that the boundary plays a role in how people respond to different kinds of drugs. These diverse findings are mentioned simply to illustrate the fact that boundary feelings may influence many aspects of behavior. The solidity or fragility you ascribe to your "base of operations" in the world permeates your life style.

What does it take to produce a person who feels that his borders are substantial and safe? We (Fisher, 1970; Fisher and Cleveland, 1968) have looked at this question in a number of studies in which we actually evaluated the parents of children who differed in boundary characteristics, but we have been able to come up with only half-formed, tentative answers. In essence, what we have found is that parents who continually intrude upon their children prevent them from constructing adequate borders. If a parent makes his child feel that he is "owned" or that he cannot function acceptably disconnected from the cord, that child apparently fails to believe in the integrity of his own body. It has been speculated by some that the child does not at first distinguish his body from that of mother. Presumably, mother and child are so close and their interaction so intimate that the child feels as if they are both part of one system. It is said that a fundamental step in his maturing is learning to distinguish his body from mother's —to become aware that his body belongs to himself. Many mothers fight this process. They are gratified in various ways by being able to experience the child's body as an extension of their own. There is safety in numbers and also in having auxiliary replicas of self close by. It has even been speculated that the reason that some women become so disturbed during the post-partum period, when they have completed their pregnancy, is that they have come to view the fetus as a part of their own body and therefore regard the passage of the child out of the vagina as a loss of their own precious body substance. So much of the mother's early relationship with the child is bodily in nature. She is constantly feeding, cleaning, and touching him, and it is likely that she can communicate her underlying feelings about "owning" him. A mother who persistently imposes her own time rhythms and standards on a child and who will not recognize the signals he gives her about when are the best times for him to have certain needs gratified is telling that child loud and clear that she does not respect him as a separate system. He is, for her, only an extension of her own wishes and needs. Such attitudes can be particularly vividly conveyed during toilet training, sleep scheduling, and making up rules about how much freedom the child can have in using his muscles to move around in space. In later years similar messages can be given in myriad ways. A mother may insist that her adolescent daughter eat certain foods. Or she may carefully scrutinize her daughter's body each time they meet and convey to her in this act that she still considers it to be an object that belongs to her and for which the daughter will have to be explicitly accountable. Or a father may demand that his son use his body only in ways that have clear phallic connotations (for example, for aggression or competitive sports) and do it in such a fashion as to communicate that he really is exploiting his son's body as an extension of his own to get satisfactions that he feels he did not get enough of in his own life.

This process by which parents use their children's bodies as extensions of their own is more direct but not grossly different from the way in which the masses symbolically exploit the bodies of certain highly publicized figures. The woman who has seen every Marilyn Monroe movie and wants to make her own body into a counterpart has really established a bond between Marilyn Monroe's body and her own. It is interesting, in this respect, that some writers have spoken of the pain and suffering experienced by persons like Marilyn Monroe because they have become aware of the degree to which they are incorporated into the self systems of others and begin to sense that they will cease to exist as significant figures unless they conform to the roles assigned to them in these systems. Marilyn Monroe may, through the expectations of her fans, have been locked into a certain way of regarding and treating her body in the same way that a child is by the body expectations of his parents. It is apropos to mention, too, that one observer (Stein, 1956) has remarked that husband and wife not infrequently treat each other's bodies as self extensions. He has described clinical examples in which a wife would fantasize that her husband's penis was her possession and as long as they were close she could attribute some of his phallic qualities to herself. In a more negative way, there are cases cited in the literature in which a man has been so identified with his wife's body that he manifests symptoms of "morning sickness" when she becomes pregnant.

The parent who over-possesses his child's body will ultimately pay severe penalties. He will discover that his child does not mature psychologically and that he demands to stay embedded in his parent's corporeal world. He becomes a parasite on the parent and one with considerable destructive power. A good example of this phenomenon is provided by the so-called "school phobia." There are children who are anxious about leaving home and going to school. Some reach the point where they are terrified about making the break each day from home base to the school world. It has become increasingly evident that in many instances this terror is really the terror of a parent (usually a lonely mother) who is so accustomed to having the child clutched close, an auxiliary self replica, that she cannot tolerate it being away. She has a large repertoire of techniques for "telling" that child that being at home close by her side is the only safe thing to do. But, of course, she is on the other hand also much disturbed by the fact that her child is behaving abnormally and expecting her to cope with his distress. I have seen dramatic improvement in the "school phobia" child as soon as the mother is made aware of the frightening signals she is giving to her child. When she stops demanding that he view his body as an extension of her own, he is relieved of his disturbance.

The child will battle to ward off intrusion into his body. He will not sleep when his mother tells him that he should. He will spit out foods that taste good to her. He will refuse to urinate and defecate at the times she schedules him to do so. Even more poignantly, it is my impression that he will defiantly experiment with destroying the body that no longer belongs to him. Children who feel owned may court accidents and risks that will damage their bodies and in so doing give the implicit message: "You may want to take over my body but I would rather destroy it than let that happen." This is the scorched-earth policy of the body realm. Similar behavior is seen in the prisoner who dramatically defies the state's ownership of his incarcerated body by mutilating it (for example, cutting a leg tendon). I would conjecture further that an analogous attitude plays a significant part in adult suicide, although I would add that there is currently no solid scientific evidence available on these points. What other things do children perhaps do to assert their body integrity? They vomit back food that has been forced into them. They revolt against the clothes that are fitted to them. They masturbate in defiance of parental expectations about what one may properly do to one's genitals. They grow beards, keep themselves dirty, eat themselves into a state of ugly obesity, and so forth. The use of drugs, with the implied message, "I put anything into my body that I please and whether you like it or not," may also be a significant technique for declaring corporeal independence, although paradoxically it can, because of the resultant addiction, lead to a much more radical loss of body independence.

Intuitively, people do learn strategies for shoring up their boundaries. As was mentioned earlier, they touch and caress themselves, soothe their skin with hot showers, wear body-embracing clothes, arrange to be held and cuddled, and so forth. But would it not be sensible to have available systematic knowledge about how to do so? I would propose that we early instruct people in the fact that they have boundary feelings that play a role in how they experience the world. They should be educated about the sensations that betoken feelings of boundary strength versus fragility. The conditions that produce boundary disturbance should be specified so that they can be avoided, if the individual so desires. We have found in our laboratory that we can exercise some control over the boundary by instructing people to focus their attention on specific body areas. For example, we can augment the boundary by getting them to increase their awareness of their skin and muscles. This can be done by deliberate control of attention or by engaging in exercises that activate skin and muscle. It is also possible to manipulate the boundary in the other direction. A person's boundaries can be rendered more vague by showing him how to focus his attention upon the interior of his body (for example, his stomach and heart). We do not yet know the potentialities of such techniques. If people systematically practiced increasing their awareness of their boundary areas day after day, could this lead to a long-term increase in the strength of the border? Could this approach be used to help children who are poorly individuated? There are already several studies that show that schizophrenic patients can be helped for brief periods to firm up their borders by being given tasks that increase their skin and muscle awareness. Several therapists (Fisher, 1970) have used body touching and body exercises to help severely disturbed children develop a greater sense of individuation and personal solidity. It is a logical step from the term *body exercise* to speculation about the potential value of various athletic activities in helping the person with an inadequate sense of boundary safety. I suspect that the gymnasium in the average school could be more than a place where kids get exercise and perfect their motor skills. In the Greek tradition of a sound body for a sound mind, I would propose that more systematic use be made of the gymnasium to provide certain kinds of body experiences that will selectively reinforce different dimensions of the body concept. All exercise is not equivalent in potential for repairing body-image defects. The child who has poor boundaries may find exercises that require unusual postures (for example, somersaults, head stands) to be disorienting and to strain his capacity for maintaining an image of himself as a bounded entity. But some steady rhythmic activity (jogging, throwing a ball back and forth, simple dance steps, for example) might create a general massaging activation of the muscles that would be comforting in its periphery-delineating effect. It is probably true that many people learn on their own, over the course of their lives, that certain forms of exercise leave them feeling particularly good. But it might take a long period of trial and error to discover just what is good. It would certainly be preferable if we could short-circuit the process and give people knowledgeable assistance in choosing specific types of body activity that would help them to compensate for their body-image defects. I strongly believe that we are now accumulating valid scientific information about body experience that in the next decade should make it possible to undertake some sensible trial efforts of the sort I have hinted at in school gymnastic settings.

An intriguing question that arises is whether average persons from various national territories differ in how they experience their body borders. Does the average German differ from the average American in this respect? Does the Frenchman differ from the Englishman? There is some evidence that such national differences may exist (Fisher and Cleveland, 1968), but a lot more research needs to be done before any confident generalizations can be offered. We (Fisher and Cleveland, 1968) uncovered such interesting tidbits as a tendency for Haitians to have less definite boundaries than persons living in the United States and for the Bhils of India to have more definite ones. One of the big problems in such evaluations is getting a measure of boundary definiteness from a sufficiently representative sample of each national group so that one can confidently speak of the average for that group. I would expect that when reliable information has finally been assembled we will find that the behaviors of nations are in some respects linked to the boundary attributes of their inhabitants. In other words, the fundamental body feeling of the average person will be an important component of how the entire nation conducts itself. It is pertinent to this point that many wars have been fought in the name of proving ethnic superiority, which is after all a declaration of a certain species of body superiority. The Aryan rally theme of the Nazis is an excellent example. In contacts with persons of different countries you can sense that they structure their boundaries differently. There are numerous little hints. One person stands very close when he is talking and another remains at an aloof distance. One touches your body to emphasize a point and another keeps his hands strictly to himself. One is overly concerned about protecting his body and another is casual about body threats. One holds his muscles stiff and ready to ward things off and another seems almost unaware of the protective possibilities of his musculature. An anthropologist (Lee, 1959) has given us unusual insight into how fantastically unlike cultures can be with respect to boundary setting. She describes one Indian group in which the individual is never thought of as a separate entity and where, in fact, their language lacks a word for "self," in the sense that this word is used in our milieu. She describes another culture in which the sense of individual boundaries is so diffuse that people do not have any of the usual compunctions about contacting each other's body secretions. When eating, they pass food around from each other's plates and even moisten pellets of food with their own saliva before exchanging them. The saliva from the mouth of another is esteemed rather than treated with disgust; it is as much valued as one's own saliva. There is a body mutuality that bypasses the usual distinction between "my body" and "your body."

Predicting the character of the link between body feeling and national behavior is tricky because there are so many other factors that intervene along the way in shaping national policies. But there are certain possibilities worth contemplating. The nation in which there is unusual concern about boundary substantiality might be expected to be particularly preoccupied with anxiety about its national borders, or unusually concerned about maintaining its ethnic purity in the face of foreign intrusion, or even preoccupied with limiting the access of its own citizens to free passage out of its borders. In actual fact, fear of body intrusion may be so universal that it is not surprising when viewing the international scene to find that alarm and conflict about national boundaries are terribly widespread. The nations with low border sensitivity are the exception. But it is probably still true that there are detectable national differences. It needs to be repeated that the view that I am expressing has its roots in the idea that the way in which a nation treats the individual bodies of its children, the amount of respect it has for the child's body as a private domain, will eventually reverberate in the gyrations of the entire national body. Margaret Mead has offered some interesting impressions of how the behavior of Balinese parents toward the bodies of their children eventuates in the children displaying certain lifelong preferences and traits. For example, the Balinese child is kept closer to his mother's body and for longer periods of time than is true in most other cultures. His world is to an unusual extent framed or defined by her body movements. Mead suggests that as a result certain of the mother's typical rhythms, such as the repetitious movements she uses in pounding rice, determine the rhythms of the music later most preferred by Balinese adults.

A final point I would like to underscore is that while each person tends in the long run to have a certain characteristic way of experiencing his body boundaries, he probably fluctuates sharply in this experience at times. He may in the course of some stressful event lose boundary delineation precipitously or in moments of unusual calm and security show a spurt in boundary accentuation. We have found in our laboratory that we can disturb the boundary by bombarding people with repetitious messages, particularly if they have hostile content (Fisher, 1970). The real events that bombard people day in and day out can also probably alter their sense of boundary security. The person who is suddenly faced with surgery or whose house burns down and who is left without a shelter he can call his own may react with the feeling that his borders are endangered and too weak to cope with the intrusions that are imminent. A city dweller who is used to moving in well-defined and hedged-in streets may feel opened up when standing in a desert area where no habitations are in sight. The lost child who feels his self dissolving in the panic of suddenly drifting into a world without recognizable landmarks just as quickly regains his self contours when Mother finds him. Each person battles day and night to maintain his borders. The struggle to maintain control over a separate chunk of the world's space does not, in some respects, seem very different from the strategies of the one-celled organism protecting itself behind its enclosing membrane.

CHAPTER
THREE

Masculine and feminine body feelings

There are few natural events that our culture so dramatizes as the differences between the male and female bodies. Children are fervently instructed about what is masculine versus what is feminine. Except for brief periods in history, much emphasis has typically been placed upon clothing the male and female bodies in such distinctly dissimilar ways that no doubt can exist of their diametrically opposite qualities. Even today, when there is so much talk of uni-sex clothing, the television screen is congested with an array of advertisements that unambiguously demarcate the feminine from the masculine things that have to do with the body. There is little question that bras, girdles, stockings, perfume, and devices for coping with menstruation belong to the realm of the womanly body. In ways too numerous to count we learn that the male body is phallic and the female body vaginal. The male is symbolized by aggressive protrusion and the female by the fact of her receptive body opening. The preoccupation with sex differences is so pervasive that in many languages all nouns are given a masculine, feminine, or neuter designation. Relatedly, one finds certain colors labeled as belonging more to one sex than the other; some foods are

41

considered to be more suited to men than women; and even the sex of God has to be unambiguously specified.

The distinction between male and female bodies is one of the most fundamental facts of life. It pervades our culture and is an ever-present intermediary. This chapter will search out the body experiences associated with masculinity and feminity. It will analyze how they enter into identity, how they influence the psychological role of the body in decision-making, and how they shape the character of one's outer façade. It will provide the opportunity to consider in depth how your masculine or feminine body sensations induce you to treat yourself and others in special ways.

When comparing the male and the female body, it does not take long to get into matters of superiority-inferiority. There is a good deal of preoccupation in our culture with the question of whether it is better to have the body of a man or of a woman. The traditional and most commonly held public view is that the masculine body is superior. But at the same time, there is a chronic, excited admiration of the female body that extends into every byway of communication and thought. The painter, the sculptor, the poet, and the movie-maker have lavished their admiration on the beautiful womanly body. I do not think that this is merely a reflection of the fact that the most influential people in these fields have been men and therefore interested in the female body as a potential sex object. As a matter of fact, many homosexual male artists have been equally invested in the vision of feminine beauty. The female body may be so lavishly focused upon because of its unique creative potential, the mystery of its cyclic alterations, the nurturant qualities it exemplifies, and so forth. These are qualities that go beyond sexual attraction as such. Today we find the female body, decked out in many costumes and guises, still the chief mode of getting advertising attention (whether it is to sell a car or to attract donations to a charitable cause), and this is true despite the fact that it is women (who from a strictly sexual viewpoint would be more interested in the male body) rather than men who are the shoppers. Generally speaking, the female form is more admired and focused upon in our communities than is the male.

However, the writings of the scientific and clinical experts uniformly give the message that the average woman has an inferior concept of her body. Freud was clear and definite in his announcement that women are universally depressed with their body inheritance. He said, on the basis of his analysis of the fantasies of women he had treated psychotherapeutically, that a woman thinks of herself as castrated and lacking an essential organ. He speculated that because the female does not have a penis, which presumably has a special superior value, she unconsciously imagines that her vagina is a rent in her body produced by some castrating procedure that deprived her of the phallus. He assumed that a woman never got over the shock of this loss and that no matter how much she compensated she always had some amount of "penis envy." She was doomed to experience her body as being of only second-rate quality. Freud's view became widely accepted and several generations of female psychiatric patients have now been treated within a context that assumes that one of their important sources of dissatisfaction is being stuck with a castrated body. While a number of female psychoanalysts (for example, Horney, 1939) have disagreed with Freud's position and pointed out that women have a great deal to be proud of with respect to their bodies (for example, the fact that only the female body can construct a new miniature human), they have not really been able to tip the scales authoritatively. Indeed, the general trend in most places is to equate the male body with strength and the female body with weakness. This is usually a simple translation of the differences in muscular strength between the two sexes. Interestingly, it ignores the well-documented fact that the female body is considerably more resistive to various body ailments and disabilities and survives longer than the male.

But what about the idea that the average woman experiences her body as inferior to that of the male? The available scientific evidence flatly contradicts it. Let us consider some of the actual pertinent observations that have been made.

I would like to begin by describing an experiment we carried out in our laboratory that involved college men and women. We asked each of them to stand in front of a mirror with his eyes closed. The room was completely dark. We then put a lifelike rubber mask on his face and instructed him to open his eyes and to be prepared to view himself in a mirror when a light flashed on. The light flashed very briefly, and he was asked to describe how his face looked. This was done a number of times. Half of the masks used portrayed male faces and half female faces. Interestingly, we discovered that the males had considerably more difficulty in identifying the female masks on their faces than did the females identifying the male masks that were placed on them. The men seemed to be much more upset about seeing their feminized mirror images than the females were in seeing their masculinized images. The reliability of these results was demonstrated when we were able to repeat them in a second study. One interpretation would be that it is more of a come-down for a man to find that he has feminine attributes than it is for a woman to find that she has masculine attributes. But I chose to focus on the apparently greater adaptability of the women in coping with an unexpected visual reversal of the sex of their physique. It seemed to me that the women were better able to cope with what amounted to a distortion in their usual physical appearance. Since the time of that experiment a pool of new information has accumulated that supports the direction of the interpretation I favored. This information takes a number of forms and shows, in general, that the average woman feels more secure about her body than does the average man. This is a heretical statement; but let us proceed to look at some of the evidence.

Several investigators who have searched the imaginative productions of children have been impressed with how often boys are preoccupied with getting hurt. For example, the spontaneous stories recounted by boys are permeated with themes of body destruction (Pitcher and Prelinger, 1963). People get stabbed, crushed, injured, and shot, and are often just at the edge of body catastrophe. Such themes are relatively rare in the spontaneous stories of girls. This difference between the sexes persists from childhood into the adult years. Even in their dreams men are more preoccupied than women with all of the nasty things that can happen to your body. Their dream characters are more often portrayed warding off body-damaging attack. The dreams of women are about friendlier vistas (Fisher, 1973). Several investigators have also observed that when people have to enter a hospital for treatment the anxiety of the male about his body under such circumstances is greater than that of the female. Relatively great concern about suffering hurt gets stirred up in the male. It has been found, too, that in families where one of the parents is chronically ill the male children get more disturbed than the female children by their persistent contact with such illness (Arnaud, 1959). In other words, there is information from several different sources that suggests that men are usually more worried about potential harm to their bodies than are women. Therefore, men can be said to be relatively more insecure about their bodies.

Formal psychological studies have added support to this view. I have shown (Fisher, 1970) that the average woman feels more secure about her body boundaries than does the average man. I have also shown that women are more open to awareness of their bodies and more likely to feel comfortable tuning in on their body sensations (Fisher, 1970). In fact, there is some evidence that while the body-aware woman is an active person with a clear image of her identity, the body-aware man is inclined to a passive-dependent orientation. Interestingly, in one of our projects (Fast and Fisher, 1971) we injected into men and women a substance (adrenalin) that produces a variety of potentially disturbing body sensations, and we discovered that the men were more discomforted by these sensations than were the women.

We have also found that men are more disturbed when they get the feeling that something has bypassed their body boundaries and gained access to their interior. We have exposed men and women to repetitive tape-recorded messages of different intensities designed to break through their defenses, and it has turned out that men are more flustered than women by the fact that these messages get through. In fact, women show almost no disruption under such circumstances (Fisher, 1970). I have offered the interpretation that a woman grows up with a basic acceptance of the idea that her body will be penetrated (during sexual intercourse) and that objects will find their way to her interior. But the average man is reared in the tradition that his body should be like a fort. It should be impregnable and anything that tries to penetrate it is dangerous.

Why should men feel less secure about the body than do women? Why should women be more comfortable than men about tuning in on their body sensations?

I think the answer can be extracted from the contrasting roles assigned to the body in the career of the average woman as compared to that of the average man. Physical strength and a handsome countenance are admired in men. Male athletic prowess is rewarded with praise and honors during the school years. But when all is said and done, there is probably little relationship between the attributes of a man's body and his chances of attaining success in life. For a man, his work and status are the prime definers of who he is and the amount of respect he will receive. There are few kinds of work left in our culture in which muscular prowess or body attractiveness help a man to succeed. Unless you are a professional athlete, there is not much prestige or reward in being strong or bodily graceful. Actually, the most prestigious male occupations are built around intellectual sharpness and cleverness. Even a man without a body could enter into such occupations! In other words, I am suggesting that the average male cannot easily grasp how his body is going to participate in the core occupational role he will assume. It is apropos to add that a recent survey has shown that middle-class women are more interested in a man's intelligence and occupational status than in his physical appearance when they look for a marriage partner. The average man is puzzled about where his body fits into the scheme of things. His body has somehow become separated from a major aspect of his aspirations. So, he feels alienated from his body and puzzled about what to do with it.

His tendency to invest more in the importance of his head than of his body was beautifully substantiated in a study by Himmelstein (1964). He asked men and women to indicate what areas of the body they most associated with self. In other words, where, in an imaginative sense, does self reside in the body? He found that men were inclined to associate self with the head and women with the chest and body area. This difference in where "self" is assigned is vividly congruent with the diminished importance that body, as such, has for men in our society.

The male attitude contrasts with what one finds to be true for the average woman. Despite Women's Liberation, it remains true that most women still perceive their life career as built around attracting a man to form a marriage alliance and then becoming pregnant and bearing children. They can trace a link directly between their body attributes and what will be their core role in life. A woman's body is in most instances an important part of how society defines her status. From an early age the female seems to be more at home with her body. Girls are authorized by the culture to experiment more with body appearance and clothing. They try out cosmetics and shift from one radical clothes style to another. But more than that, they are given the freedom to invest great energy and attention in the body. A girl who sits for a long period of time in front of the mirror studying her appearance and fussing with new body variations is doing the conventional thing. If a boy were to focus his attention on his body in a similarly direct way he would be regarded as queer or deviant. A boy can cultivate the strength of his body, but he is not supposed to demonstrate any signs of straight, unfettered, self-scanning narcissism. A Dutch psychologist (van Lennep, 1957) has found not only that boys are less aware of their bodies than are girls but also that this difference is accentuated as the two sexes pass into adulthood.

There is another important reason why the female faces up to her body in a more meaningful way than the male does. Despite myths about feminine delicacy, largely promulgated by men, it is the women in the world who are brought most intimately into contact with body phenomena that have negative and often disgusting connotations.

Women are taught to be the caretakers of the body. Their education in how to cope directly with the real body is strongly initiated by their own menstrual cycle. A woman has to adapt to a recurrent flow of blood out of her body. The uncontrolled escape of blood from a body opening is a fact of life for her and she has to assimilate this repeated experience into her body concept. She also has to assimilate an image of her body as an entity that will some day contain a child and in the process be radically changed in size and appearance—finally discharging liquids, blood, and child in the ritualized public arena of the hospital delivery room. Not only do most women arrive at a keen awareness of these facts, but they also come to view them in a positive and even honorific fashion. Even though women complain about the discomfort of an experience like menstruation, there is good evidence that they regard it as a positive badge of their femininity and mourn its loss when fate forces the removal of the uterus (Fisher, 1973).

It should be added that women also get more exposure to body phenomena in their role as food preparers. They are the ones who deal with food in its raw form. They actually see the dead chicken, the blood on the meat, the eviscerated form, and the cracked egg emitting its embryonic content. The male more typically sees only the finished product—cooked, coated, and prettified in a way that often conceals its organic origins.

Relatedly, each woman knows that the role of mother centers on the care of children. This means she will get intimately involved with the secretions and outputs of her child's body. She learns that she will be expected to deal with the urine and feces coming from the body of another. It is well known that men are much more reluctant to change diapers and make intimate contact with the body of the child than is the mother. There is a good deal of humor about such matters in the middle-class household. The role of female in our society calls for the ability to feel positively toward body phenomena that have negative connotations. It is the woman who is the nurse in most cultures. One can argue that this merely represents the assignment of a depreciated role to her, but I would guess that an important element in her being the nurse is that she feels more comfortable about coping with the stark chemical events of the body. It is true that physicians face up to similar events, but they do so in a more specialized way and with less chance of "getting dirty." They channel their body ministrations through the nurse. The greater realism of the female's body orientation was nicely illustrated by the findings of one study (Katcher, 1955) that little girls have a more accurate knowledge of the differences between the female and male genitals than do boys. This was partially traced to the fact that girls and their mothers are more open and free about displaying their bodies to each other than are boys and their fathers.

For the woman, the body is the matrix for most major events. This is not true for the man. Increasingly, his universe derives from what his brain and head can accomplish. He is even taught by the culture that it is bad to look too much in the direction of his own body. The male's woes about body things have been reinforced by his puzzlement concerning the amazing events he secretly glimpses in the woman's body. He hears about menstruation and pregnancy and breasts that enlarge to produce milk but has few opportunities to make direct eye contact with them. They remain mysterious and alien, and as a result men have invented elaborate myths about the evil and dirt inherent in female physiology. The female who directly witnesses the blood coming out of her body has a realistic, and after a while even a bored awareness of what is happening and so does not, like the male, have to carry around a lot of weird notions about basic body processes.

Mention should also be made of the simple difference between what the two sexes are led to expect about attack on their bodies. Perhaps men have more body anxiety because they have been socialized around the theme that they are fighters and defenders who must learn to use the body in combat. If you are schooled to be a warrior you will naturally expect that someone will eventually attack you with a dangerous weapon. Women are not expected to be warriors or to fight. They do not have to grow up with the idea that they will inevitably get involved in combat. It is true that girls are given the message that unfriendly men might try to exploit them sexually. Anxiety about rape is promulgated in our culture. But I would maintain that the woman's fear of being aggressively penetrated is relatively minor in comparison to her wish to be penetrated. As a matter of fact, several studies suggest that women have a way of erotizing even aggression displayed toward them. Women were found to experience aggression as having sexually arousing properties significantly more often than men do. Even the image of death had erotic overtones to women (Fisher, 1973).

Aside from the issue of body security, what other ways do the male and female body-images differ?

Obviously, one of the prime contrasts relates to the phallic versus vaginal orientation. It derives from the simple fact of the male possessing a penis and the female a vagina (and all of the associated learning that goes along with having a male rather than a female body). The difference is so fundamental that it permeates the fantasies and perceptions of the two sexes. For example, if you ask males and females to take toy blocks and other materials and to construct a scene, the males will more often build in phallic qualities. They will more often create towers and upright structures. Contrastingly, women will more often portray interior spaces and the accesses in and out of these spaces. Similar differences have been demonstrated when men and women are asked to complete certain standard drawings. The men will significantly more often compose the completions that are upright or protrusive.

Men identify masculinity with being large, and women identify femininity with being small. When women are asked how they would most like to alter their own bodies, they often mention reducing the size of various anatomical parts. Their only aspiration for largeness emerges with reference to their breasts (Fisher, 1970). Generally, they equate the feminine body with an image of miniaturization. The Chinese once carried this image to the extreme by insisting that girls bind their feet and come to adulthood with feet that were truly miniature ones—so small they could not be functionally used. At the other extreme, the male wants his body to make an impression of muscular largeness. He wants it to loom powerfully in the visual space.

The phallic body orientation also importantly involves the feeling that your body can move easily and swiftly. The male hero is often portrayed as having to traverse great distances or having to get from one place to another in record speed in order to accomplish his mission. Women have, in most cultures, been assigned a stationary role. They are supposed to stay put. They are taught to be fearful of motility. Analysis of the dreams of the two sexes has shown that those of men more often involve swift mastery of space. I have found in some of my work that women actually have more anxiety about their legs, which are the means to motility, than do men (Fisher, 1970). I would speculate that this will rapidly change and that in another generation motility and speed will no longer be alien to the feminine body concept. The fact that it is becoming widely acceptable for women to hitchhike and to drive at high speed is evidence of the changing perspective toward the woman moving independently in space.

Of course there is also the obvious male-female difference linked to the fact that the female body becomes the site for reproduction and the container of the developing fetus. We do not really know how much the average woman carries around an image of this aspect of her body, but one would speculate that she does, indeed, focus on her pregnancy potential. We actually know, as earlier mentioned, that women attach great importance to their menstrual cycles and come to regard menstruation as a positive badge of their femininity. This is true despite the problems and inconveniences associated with the monthly flow of blood. Women who suffer the loss of the uterus as the result of surgery mourn the resulting loss of the menstrual process. Interviews with such women have shown that menstruation becomes a vital part of their body image. The monthly cycle becomes a repetitive validation of their femininity. There is even evidence that some women find in the menstrual experience a reassurance about their feminine identity that results in greater ego integration. One study has found that schizophrenic women have better ego integration during menstruation than at other times (Fisher, 1970).

It is noteworthy that despite the fact that the two sexes are so anatomically different it is difficult, beyond the few gross matters just cited, to specify the differences in the ways they experience their bodies. One can only point vaguely to the involvement of such factors as phallic versus non-phallic qualities, total degree of body awareness, potentiality for producing and containing the developing child, and the meaningfulness of the body to the individual's total life role. We have a lot more to learn about such issues. For example, we know little about how most women feel about their breasts and the role they play in feminine self-definition. How much awareness of her breasts does the average woman have? What has been the effect of the fact that so many women have ceased to breast-feed and that the breasts have become primarily objects of display rather than functionally meaningful organs? Puzzling inconsistencies are found with respect to breast display. It has been pointed out that although women in the lower socioeconomic groups are more likely to use clothing and devices that starkly emphasize the breasts, it is in this socioeconomic group that breast stimulation as a part of foreplay is relatively de-emphasized (Jesser, 1971). There is also the interesting fact that breast display results in an emphasis on body protuberance that is supposed to be a phallic quality. Why should one of the most widely accepted representations of the female body go in the direction of emphasizing protuberance? One would have thought that the concave, receptive aspects of the female body would be the most advertised. Similar kinds of questions could be raised about almost any of the body attributes that distinguish male and female.

It was earlier pointed out that the average woman is relatively more aware of her body than is the average man. She keeps tuning in on her body to a greater extent. The male pays less attention to his own body and more to other objects. Because this is so women might be expected to be more influenced than men are by body feelings when responding to situations. For example, a woman might be more likely to choose one alternative just because it "feels" better to her than does some other alternative. Or she might prefer one book or artistic production to another just because she reacts more positively to it in terms of her body sensations. A man might be inclined to ignore (or be unaware of) his body sensations and to look to a more cognitive or logical basis for his decision. This fits in with the widely accepted stereotype that holds that women are more emotional and less logical than men. In other words, the woman's greater sensitivity to body cues is given a negative significance. However, I would like to point out that body feelings may not infrequently be a better guide to action than are carefully teased out chains of logic. Feelings of body pleasantness or unpleasantness may derive from very fundamental matters of fit or lack of fit between an individual and his environment. Reason may tell a person that it is to his advantage to pursue some job or task until it is completed, but his body feelings may more importantly tell him that such a job is potentially threatening to his health or psychologically dehumanizing. A carefully reasoning man may choose to work for a particular boss on the basis of the money and prestige that will be derived, but all the while his uncomfortable body may be telling him that such a boss will be a constant emotional threat to him and ultimately elicit serious disturbance. I have proposed in another book (Fisher, 1970) that most of the child's early contacts with the world are in terms of body feelings and that he learns to like or not like certain things in relation to how much body discomfort they arouse in him. During these early years he trusts the advice from his body and gets to know a lot of situations through their corporeal repercussions. He stores up a lot of fairly wise lore about what is good for him. But as he matures, especially if he is male, he is taught to ignore this lore and to rely more on what his brain computes to be rational. He is systematically trained to turn away from body evaluations. Women seem not to be so pressed on this issue, or if they are they somehow manage to put up more resistance. They continue to turn to their body experiences as an important source of guidance. The greater "emotionality" of women is one manifestation of their greater closeness to (and less inhibitory stance toward) the shifting patterns of sensations pulsing through their bodies.

The average woman seems to be able to relate to her body more flexibly than does the male. An obvious example of this fact is the swift way in which women can shift from one clothing fashion to another. Women are constantly experimenting with ways of altering their appearance. While men now show greater willingness to try out new fashions than they once did, the fact remains that they do so to a much smaller extent than is true of women. A more spectacular example is provided by the frequency with which women and men seek optional plastic surgery. By optional is meant surgery to improve one's appearance but not occasioned by some gross deformity produced by injury or disease. A much larger percentage of women than of men are willing to take a chance on a gross reshaping of some part of their anatomy in order to become more visually attractive. In fact, the relatively rare man who does seek plastic surgery has been found to be rather deviant and psychologically more troubled than the average. In a series of studies carried out in my laboratory (Fisher, 1970) we have found that women have a less fixed and regular way of looking at their bodies than men do. If you systematically inquire about where on their bodies people focus their attention, you find a tendency for consistency. One person is habitually particularly aware of his head, another of his arms, another of the back rather than the front of his body, and so forth. But what surprised us about the findings we obtained is that women are less consistent than men in these patterns of body awareness. A woman may be particularly focused upon her head one day but not the next. However, a man who has high awareness of his head one day tends to display the same pattern of awareness at a future time. It is possible that the average woman has to learn to maintain a more flexible attitude toward her body than does the man because of the menstrual cycle and her potential for becoming pregnant. That is, she repeatedly experiences rather profound changes in the feel of her body as her menstrual cycle waxes and wanes. She finds the patterns of her body experience in continual transition and so cannot have one fixed way of perceiving herself. Also, she learns from an early age that her body has a pregnancy potential that could eventuate in profound alterations in the size and other attributes of her body. In other words, not only is she exposed to regular body change but she expects, as part of her life career, that she will experience the gross body shifts that occur during pregnancy. There is no comparable set of experiences for the male. Following the changes of adolescence his body remains fairly unaltered for decades, and he can anticipate only the gradual alterations that accompany aging. He can adopt rather rigid modes of viewing his body, which have already been encouraged earlier by the fact that the male is not supposed to devote much self-conscious attention to his body or to experiment much with its appearance. He is supposed to leave his body alone.

A fascinating question arises as to why women seem driven to experiment so much with their appearance. If they have to experience more changes in their bodies than men do simply because of their biological makeup, why do they seek even more change? One might think that they would try to counter the repeated alterations they are exposed to by adopting practices that would minimize other kinds of body experience shifts. From this view, they might be expected to be even more resistive to fashion changes than men are.

It is not easy to arrive at a satisfactory perspective on this puzzle. Various possibilities come to mind. One could argue that the eagerly sought-after changes in the woman's fashion world are reflections of continuous womanly biological changes. Women may simply be acting out in their public clothing changes the private sense of being in bodily flux. There might be a need in women to give public validation or public meaning to their fluctuating body sensations. The fashion changes would represent an institutionalized way for women to support each other. It would be a channel for externalizing in public ceremony what is each woman's private feeling. But essentially it would be a way of declaring, "It is right and proper for a woman to have different feelings about her body at different times, and we declare this to be true by the fact that we expect her to keep changing her bodily appearance and clothing style."

Another way of looking at the woman's eagerness to revamp her appearance is that it represents an attempt at mastery of body events that are disturbing. She may find it distressing to be exposed to such radical cycles in body feeling. She may develop doubts about the stability of her body as a home base. To compensate for this and to reassure herself she may seize upon deliberate frequent alteration of her appearance. In so doing, she is asserting, "I am not afraid of body change. In fact, I instigate such change in myself. If there is a lot of shift in how my body feels, it is because I keep doing things to my body that alter it. I cause the changes. Therefore, I am really in charge of them."

Still another interpretation, but one more positive in flavor, would be that women direct their creativity into the body world. They get a lot of expert and sophisticated experience with the body and know their way around in this realm. But at the same time, there are all kinds of societal restrictions on their gaining access to outside jobs and roles where they have the chance to innovate and be creative. So, they invest creativity in new ways of presenting and experiencing the body. They pioneer in new perspectives on their own bodies. They approach their body topography with some of the same zest for novelty as is shown by the explorer who is looking for new territories. There is, of course, a good deal of secondary reward to the woman whose body innovating renders her more attractive to men. The zest for body innovating is quickened by the potential sexual and sex-role rewards that are promised to those who are most successful in their efforts.

It is even possible that the average man gets important satisfactions from the woman's experiments with her body not only because he wants her to attain optimum attractiveness but also because he is fascinated by the body plasticity displayed. He can, without any threat to his own frame, watch the ways in which the body can be transformed. Just as we watch acrobats and athletes for the pure fun of seeing the extreme things the body can do, the average man may monitor the latest womanly fashion transformations. Perhaps he gets some element of security from witnessing another representative of the species live with, and even enjoy, body changes that are far more extreme than he would ever try out on his own body. His body seems, then, by comparison, so much more protected and under his own control.

It may be pertinent to this point that one of the classic spectacles involving women in the United States is the strip tease. This is a situation in which men watch a woman as she removes her clothing, but all the while she is dancing and trying to surprise the audience with novel techniques for suddenly shedding this or that piece of her costume. Obviously, one of the prime motivations in watching her is to catch a glimpse of her in the nude. But I wonder if there is not also a good deal of less conscious fascination with watching her body as it changes from one state to another—from covered to uncovered, from conventionally acceptable to illicit. There are further kinds of body asymmetry introduced as she uncovers one side of the body or reveals more of the upper half than of the lower half of the body. In other words, the strip teaser represents the female body in a state of exciting change, and the chance to confront such a vivid change experience in the body realm may be a significant component of the satisfaction derived from watching her. Body alteration is a universal problem and challenge. It means many things, but one of the most fundamental has to do with the unavoidable changes in the body that accompany the normal life cycle. To witness the body becoming altered, whether it be in the form of a baby growing larger or of someone trying on a new exotic costume, is to become involved with issues of body transformation and all of the derivative implications about development, aging, and decline. Of course the degree to which such implications are important will depend upon the age and body security of the witness. But ultimately all persons find such themes taking on significance.

The experiments that the average woman conducts with her own bodily appearance have some of the elements of camouflage. Women use cosmetics and clothes to conceal some things and to highlight others. There is the sense of constructing a façade. Many women refer to the application of cosmetics as "putting on a face." The camouflage intent is even more apparent in older women who apply modern technology to blotting out wrinkles and concealing gray hair. One can ask why women are so much more likely than men to camouflage their body defects. Men are still quite reluctant to cover their body deficiencies. It is simply not manly to do so. One obvious explanation of the woman's greater need to camouflage herself is that she is more clearly equated with her body than a man is with his body. The body appearance of a woman advertises roughly her status in the world of love, sex, and appeal to men. This is still a prime definer of womanly worth. But there is probably little correlation between a man's physical attractiveness and his role status. His worth is actually defined by his power or money or intellectual prowess. Even his self-definition is more related to his social status than to his appearance (excluding the presence of some serious or disfiguring body defect). A woman's self-definition is, by contrast, very likely to be heavily influenced by what she sees in the mirror.

The energetic camouflaging in which the female engages may possibly be traced to still another factor. Douvan and Adelson (1966) have found that young women are inclined to postpone the crystallization of values and attitudes until they marry and then to do so in a way that will minimize conflict with the husband. They try to avoid commitment to any extreme characterological position and to remain open to modifying self to fit with the expectations of a potential mate. In other words, they are prepared to shift roles and self-definitions. They are ready to try multiple roles, rather than a single, fixed one. Their camouflaging skills may be an expression of this attitude. Just as an actor who shifts from one part to another needs to use makeup skillfully in order to fit himself to each part, so a woman may need to use her camouflaging skills to fit herself to the roles she adopts. In one role she may need to accentuate certain of her body attitudes and in another she may have to de-emphasize them. The fact that the female tries on different roles to a greater extent than the male is apparent even in childhood. Several observers have noted that girls are more likely to attempt doing masculine things and playing with masculine toys than boys are to explore the world of femininity. Girls seem to have more freedom in contemplating what it would be like to be a boy than boys do to consider the feel of being feminine. One psychologist (McClelland, 1964) has suggested that an outstanding characteristic of women in our culture is that they are skilled at investing themselves meaningfully in a *variety* of activities.

The person who is confused about sexuality and sexual identity will often express this in the way he thinks about his body and also in the manner in which he publicizes it to others. There are cases in the psychiatric literature in which a woman delusionally acquires a penis. There are cases, too, of men who delusionally menstruate or even achieve a pregnant state. The male transvestite who feels compelled to dress up in women's clothing is obviously trying for a public transformation of the sex of his body. There are also, of course, women who for analogous reasons don male apparel. Less dramatic and less pathological techniques are used by normal people to express feelings about the sexual attributes of the body. Little is known scientifically about such phenomena, and I can only offer some of my own speculations that seem pertinent. Women who have male aspirations and who envy the phallic qualities of the male body may evidence their orientation in a number of ways. One primary technique is to enhance apparent body size. The idea of being big is peculiarly masculine. A woman may dramatize her size by wearing very full, voluminous clothing that creates an impression of expansive area. She may adopt upward-protrusive hair styles that increase her height; piling up a great deal of hair on her head (aided by various mechanical devices) can create an image of a massive head, which has giant-like connotations. It is apropos to mention that there are cases in the clinical literature in which women have been found to eat large quantities as a way of making themselves look big and aggressive. The use of high heels to elevate a woman's body is, of course, well known. Phallic qualities may also be accentuated by wearing clothing that emphasizes the long line of the thigh and leg and, by implication, the theme of motility. It has been suggested by some that displaying the breasts in a fashion that highlights their taut, outthrust character is metaphorically phallic. The male can obviously wear clothing in a way that advertises his interest in identifying with the female body. He can play down his own phallic attributes: emphasize his smallness and fragility and draw attention to the receptive as compared to the protrusive stance of his body. He can declare his dislike of motility by moving with short mincing steps and calling attention to the delicacy of his muscular output.

The upsurge of the machine, which gives great power even to the weakest of human frames, probably significantly blurs old definitions of the male and female bodies. Strength and power were typically associated with the male body, and the male body was considered to be much more capable of accomplishing certain tasks. Now, a woman with a machine has a "body" potentially more powerful than any man's. Furthermore, as machines become ever-present and familiar they seem almost to be body companions—intimately identified with our own musculature. So, the woman who has an assortment of gadgets producing substitute energy for her is probably tempted to feel as if their power is her own. She feels that her body shares in the power of the machine and in this sharing begins to compare favorably with what the male body can muster.

Apropos of this topic, I would like to call attention to the seemingly paradoxical idea that when the male and female engage in intimacy they may blur their differentiation. This idea derives from two factors. First of all, when people are intimately close they adopt attitudes and styles of behavior from each other; their closeness generates influential cross-communication and mutual influence. In a really highly sex-differentiated society, there is a good deal of sex segregation, which reduces intimacy between the sexes to a minimum. An example of how closeness of the sexes affects sex-role attitude is provided by recent studies that show that a father or a son living in a family in which there is a large feminine contingent will be influenced to adopt a feminine orientation to a greater degree than average. Similarly, a girl with numerous brothers may adopt the values of the surrounding male bloc. Secondly, and more speculatively, it is possible that body intimacy between the sexes, at the same time that it is an expression of heterosexuality, encourages identification with the body of the partner. The merging that occurs during intercourse may be threatening to some who are uncertain of their own sexual identification simply because it involves "mixing" with another category of body that they have conceptually tried to avoid. The closeness interferes with the sense of sex separateness they have sought to maintain. It is an obvious fact that whenever two cultures meet or undertake intensive commerce they begin to influence each other and ultimately to become more similar; this is probably also true with regard to intimacy and body closeness between the sexes. In the psychoanalytic literature, too, it has been asserted that disturbance about the sexual attributes of one's body is not infrequently aroused by intimate knowledge of the body of the opposite sex. For example, the view has been expounded that when a male views the female genitalia he is confronted by the inescapable fact that it is possible to be human and yet not to possess a penis. Instead of a penis there is an opening into the body. It is conjectured that if a male is insecure about the sexual qualities of his own body the perception of women as "lacking" a penis may signal to him that he, too, could suffer such a lack. The possibility of his not possessing one of the prime definers of his sexual identity becomes a concrete event in the world, one that has already happened to someone else. Presumably, the shock effect of discovering that there are humans without penises is particularly great in the case of the young male child who is only beginning to shape up a sense of masculine identity. From Freud's perspective, the female child who becomes intimately aware of the phallic anatomy of the male responds with the disturbing fantasy that she must have once possessed a similar anatomical feature but lost it as the result of some kind of castrating attack on her body. These formulations have been around in the psychoanalytic literature for a long time. They are interesting and intriguing, but they are as yet no closer to scientific verification than they were in their original Viennese setting.

I am impressed with the role of violence and aggression in maintaining a sense of distinction between what is masculine and what is feminine. Aggressive acting-out is considered to be a mark of the masculine mode. It is strongly associated with the phallic image. I would speculate that when a man has arrived at serious doubts about whether his body "feels" masculine he may be driven to an act of violence as a way of dramatically re-establishing his masculinity. The angry, thrusting, attacking use of the musculature gives nice, reassuring feedback. An interesting finding that corroborates this speculation has been provided by cross-cultural studies dealing with the relationship between "delinquent" aggressive acting-out in boys and the amount of closeness they had with their mothers while growing up. It has been found that boys who have been relatively close to their mothers and distant from their fathers (or often without a father because of his death) and who therefore have had limited opportunity to learn directly about the "feel" of being masculine have a strong need during adolescence to engage in hostile, predatory behavior as a way of announcing that they are indeed of the male species. It is well known, too, that male delinquents come with unusual frequency from broken homes in which there is no visible father and where almost all of the primary socialization experiences have been with women. The male who grossly doubts his masculinity feels compelled to turn his body into a metaphorical missile or torpedo. There can be no doubt of the sex of a destructive missile. Confusion about the sexual characteristics of one's body seems to be particularly common in seriously disorganized persons (schizophrenics, for example). Whether this confusion plays an etiological role in their disorganization is not known, but several investigators have reported that schizophrenic men and women have distorted ideas about the sexual aspects of their bodies. It is not simply a matter of their having less accurate knowledge about the nature of male and female sexual anatomy; one study demonstrated that schizophrenic patients have as much knowledge about the literal facts of sexuality and sexual anatomy as do normal persons. Rather, the distortions have to do with feelings about their bodies. There is evidence that the female schizophrenic experiences her body as if it were more masculine than it should be, and the male as if his were more feminine than is normal in males (McClelland and Watt, 1968).

Certain parts of the body are seen as more masculine or more feminine. This is obvious for the genital areas and for the breasts in women, and there is also fair agreement in designating less clearly sex-labeled sectors as being masculine or feminine (Nash, 1958; McClelland and Watt, 1968). For example, the ears, back, and elbow have been particularly judged as masculine, while the lips, face, and skin have been judged as specifically feminine in their connotations. Some disagreement does exist as to how to label the legs and fingers. It has been proposed by psychoanalytic theorists that all projecting parts of the body that are metaphorically phallic have masculine significance. Conversely, all body openings, which presumably have a metaphorical relationship to the vaginal channel, are said to have feminine meaning. There are case histories in the literature in which persons seem to express conflict about their sexual identity by becoming preoccupied with a body area that has special masculine or feminine implications. One of the most frequently cited involves the paranoid schizophrenic male who develops all kinds of delusional ideas about his back and anus. He may verbalize fantasies about machines that are doing things "in back" of him and even introducing malevolent substances into his body via the rectum. Freud speculated that such fantasies actually expressed a disguised, forbidden, homosexual wish on the part of the man to make intimate contact with another male, who would insert his penis into his rectum (which, as a body opening, could represent a substitute for the vagina). I have shown in my work (Fisher, 1970) that the two sexes do, indeed, often assign unlike meaning to the same body territories, even when they are not linked in any direct way with secondary sex characteristics. Men and women really do differ in their attitudes toward such regions as the heart, head, and eyes. To illustrate this point, let me say that there is experimental evidence that heightened head awareness is associated in women with inhibition of heterosexual impulses, but in men it is associated with concern about being able to control hostile, besmirching, and negativistic tendencies.

It remains a matter of mystery how variations in clothing fashions that shift in highlighting first one body landmark and then another may be tied to the special meanings assigned to major body regions by men and women. If women's fashions call attention to the legs at one time but to the head at another, or if they draw the spectator's eyes to the front of the pelvis today and to the buttocks tomorrow, it is likely that there are corresponding values being communicated about what may be significant to women at that time. Certain superficial deductions can be made, and at times it is clear from a woman's clothing style that she is conveying images of aggression or passivity or receptivity or desexualization. But beyond such gross interpretations, it is probable that further study will reveal more subtle correlates of what a particular clothing style emphasizes. As was mentioned earlier, we do know that a woman who wants to affirm the stability of her own personal boundaries may wear clothing that is reassuring in its highly visible (for example, check designs) swathing of the outside of the body. A woman who minimizes the visual vividness of her body and at the same time uses cosmetics to impart centrality to her head may be declaring her dedication to cognitive, intellectual (head) control and avoidance of indulgence of "body" passion. Or another woman who carefully keeps her arms covered may be signaling her reluctance to "reach out" and establish contact with others. These are only fanciful formulations on my part; we lack dependably scientific information about such matters. It is even more difficult to speculate about how men may utilize clothing styles to convey feelings and values. The tight collar, the flashy tie, and the padded exaggeration of the shoulders may each contain its own meaning. However, it is interesting that one study (Cantril and Allport, 1933) of clothing preferences found no relationship between a man's interest in clothing and his personal values, while in the case of women there were significant correlations. It may be that because the average man is less likely than his female counterpart to equate his identity with his body, he is also less likely to express important attitudes and feelings through the style in which he clothes that body.

If the average woman sees a clearer equation between her iden- ty and her body than does the average man, what are some of the implications of this proposition?

First of all, one might presume that the male feels less unified with his body. He is perhaps more likely to experience it as a shadow tagging along. He is less sure what to do with it or how it fits in with the action. He might be compared to the actor who can execute a role well in the dramatic sense but who is uncertain that his physical appearance contributes much to the performance. Secondly, it can also be conjectured that a man will more often feel that the way he looks to others does not mirror his true self. Because his bodily appearance is not equated with self as much as it is in the case of the woman, he is more likely to feel that his outer appearance is superficial and not representative of his larger character. It would be interesting to know if people do, in general, take this view and whether they consequently render judgments about men and women on a different basis. Are they more likely to judge what a woman is like from her outer appearance than they would a man? One wonders, too, if the male, because he feels that his body does not directly reflect his real self, also feels unusually deceptive or devious in his contacts with others. That is, he may feel that what others see is not an honest replica of himself. On the other hand, this point needs to be balanced against the fact that women are more likely than men to put on cosmetic and clothing façades to suit their wishes about how they want to appear to the spectator. In that more limited sense, women may more frequently feel that they are putting on a deceptive front. However, I would add the thought that women seem quickly to adapt to their cosmetic façades. They may swiftly balance the external façades against their inner self-feelings and arrive at an integration that eliminates sensations of disparity. Men may be less skilled at coping with the disparity, or one could argue that they would be more skilled because they are more accustomed to the idea that their body appearances depart from their self-images. It is difficult to reason through this issue, but I am pushed in the direction of seeing men as less skilled by the results of the experiment I described earlier in which men and women looked at themselves in the mirror while wearing incongruous masks. It was the men who showed themselves to be most alarmed and uncomfortable about the strangeness of their outer façades.

The idea is farfetched, and yet intriguing to contemplate, that men may be more invested than women in actively seeking certain very specific kinds of body satisfaction because they get less *general* body satisfaction. It has, for example, been a tradition in our society for men to pursue with special intensity the accumulation of sexual satisfaction. Women are typically seen as less focused on the pursuit of sexual relief. If this difference is a real one, does it mirror the fact that women keep accumulating body satisfactions as part of their overall "body" life-style, while men are relatively deprived in this respect and so try to extract as much as possible out of any specific mode of body satisfaction that becomes available? Men may be relatively more dependent upon a biologically triggered and focused body need to provide the opportunity for meaningful body experiences. This idea has been indirectly suggested by some commentators who have pointed out that while men seem to be interested in sex primarily as a means of relieving specific tensions, women experience sexuality as part of a larger context that will involve their bodies in producing and nurturing a child—and in fulfilling the long-term concept that the feminine body has "arrived" when it finally becomes the site for a fertilized egg.

The scientific data that have accumulated leave no doubt that men and women experience their bodies in radically unlike ways. The differences between them are not only the obvious anatomical ones, but also those of a more general nature—most essentially, in the role that the body plays in building an identity and judging life events.

CHAPTER
FOUR

Unpredictable body and the dirty stranger

Black skin and white skin, long head and wide head, short nose and long nose oppose each other in the body world. Different ethnic and racial groups stand righteously prepared to defend the superiority of their own body attributes and to mock those "not-like-me" ones that they perceive in others. I would seriously like to propose that racial prejudice gets part of its momentum from our fear of any human body that departs much from the appearance of our own.

Most of us really do get disturbed when we see someone with a body noticeably deviant from the norm. Just a moment of introspection will tell you about the upsurge of tension that gripped you at your last encounter with an amputee or a badly scarred face or a Thalidomide baby or even with the two-headed Martian featured in the science-fiction saga you recently watched on television. The assertion that anxiety is evoked by seeing a different kind of body is not merely speculation; it has been documented in the psychological laboratory. One study I would like to cite (Wittreich and Radcliffe, 1955) made ingenious use of the properties of distorting (aniseikonic) lenses. These lenses, when placed over the eyes, make it possible to perceive the world as peculiarly altered. They can make objects appear to change in size, shape, and spatial position. What is interesting and unique about them is that they have the greatest distorting effect when an individual is looking at something not threatening to him and least effect when he is viewing an object that is frightening. The anxiety generated when gazing at something threatening seems to make the individual hold on to the safety of the way things usually look and to reject the distorted perspective offered by the lenses. In the study I wish to describe it was found that when persons looked through the aniseikonic lenses at someone who was disguised to resemble an amputee who had lost an arm he appeared less distorted than someone without any body damage. In other words, the sight of the "amputee" was sufficiently disconcerting to inhibit the lens effect. It is my speculation that the sight of the amputee is alarming because it proclaims an image of a human frame lacking an arm and in so doing implies that the same loss could potentially afflict any person's body. It is not easy to attain the idea that your body is a dependable, stable entity, and yet it is fundamental to security. Unless you trust your flesh-and-blood "base of operations" you are adrift without shelter—exposed. The difficulties in arriving at a sense of residing in a stable body have to do with such things as the potentially body-damaging forces (for example, automobile injury, atomic blasts) that surround us, the radical fluctuations in body feelings that occur as we grow up from an organism weighing only a few pounds to one weighing over a hundred pounds, and the stress of changing from a state of mature tissue-resiliency to that of declining old age. A sense of body stability is hard won and probably requires a good deal of defensive shutting of your eyes to what is going on "out there." So, when you come upon a dwarf or any other variety of distorted body that is starkly there and proclaims the possibility of grossly altering the body, it shocks your fairly vulnerable body concept.

I have highlighted this point in order to lead into the view, which I have already briefly mentioned, that race prejudice is to some extent an expression of the individual's fear of a body that looks different from his own. I should emphasize that I am perfectly aware that race prejudice is a complicated phenomenon in which economic and historical factors are centrally important. But I would urge that body feelings also play a role.

The passionate hatred that Hitler displayed for Jews could be conceptualized as at least in part a defense against the alien and frightening body appearance they presented to him. Note Hitler's description (Hitler, 1939, p. 59) of an incident that set him off on his obsessive and vitriolic anti-Semitic preoccupation:

> One day, when passing through the Inner City, I suddenly encountered a phenomenon in a long caftan and wearing black sidelocks. My first thought was: Is this a Jew? . . . the longer I gazed at this strange countenance and examined it section by section, the more the question shaped itself in my brain: Is this a German?

Note also his preoccupation with Jewish dirtiness and the body imagery he uses in describing it (Hitler, 1939, p. 60):

> Was there any shady undertaking, any form of foulness, especially in cultural life, in which at least one Jew did not participate? On putting the probing knife carefully to that kind of abscess one immediately discovered, like maggots in a putrescent body, a little Jew who was often blinded by the sudden light.

He also writes of "the nightmare vision of the seduction of hundreds of thousands of girls by repulsive, crooked-legged Jewish bastards." His description of Jews as "crooked-legged" reveals his perception of them as people with grotesque, distorted bodies. It is, incidentally, apropos to mention that in various descriptions of Hitler's appearance during young manhood (Bullock, 1962) one detects the theme that the physical impression he made upon others was strange and peculiarly deviant. The following description was given of him at the age of twenty-one (Bullock, 1962, p. 34):

> He wore an ancient black overcoat . . . which reached down over his knees. From under a greasy, black derby hat, his hair hung long over his coat collar. His thin and hungry face was covered with a black beard above which his large staring eyes were the only prominent feature.

One of his acquaintances referred to his appearance as "an apparition such as rarely occurs among Christians." It is ironic that Hitler was later to become fascinated with the alien non-German (non-Christian?) attributes of the Jew. The blackness of his overcoat that impressed the observer who described him reverberates with the "black sidelocks" of the Jew whom he described in the encounter in the Inner City that he says turned him vehemently to attacking Jews.

The person whose body is sheathed in a white skin is startled when he first encounters another "kind" of person whose body is wrapped in black, and vice versa. The startlement produced by such differences is most obvious when young children are involved. They are much more spontaneous in their puzzlement. A psychiatrist named

McDonald (1970) who carefully observed the interactions of young black and white children in a school setting offers numerous examples of their comments, in which they seemed to be trying to understand how one kind of human could be bodily different from another kind. In an amusing and poignant instance she tells how, after making the proper arrangements for observation, children of one color were surprised to find that children of another color had genital structures that were not different from their own. It seemed as if they had first concluded that anyone whose skin color was so unlike their own had to have a radically different form of body. The black and white kids in this school were frightened by their skin differences. The idea that it is scary to know that your body *could* be "different" was highlighted in another incident related by McDonald. She notes that on one occasion a four-year-old white girl went on vacation and then returned with a deep tan. There were immediate signs that her classmates were disturbed about the alteration that had occurred in her skin color. They seemed to be anxious about it and for a while kept their distance from her. McDonald conjectured that they were disturbed by the idea that a person's body can change color—can be transformed. Such an idea means that your own body is not as stable and safe as you might imagine it to be. McDonald suggests that differences in skin color are especially disturbing to children because so many of their comforting and self-defining experiences with their parents involve skin contact. A child's skin is an important plane of interaction, and as part of the process of building up a picture of his relationships with others he has had to arrive at some fairly definite conclusions about its properties. The "good" skin where you get touched and where you feel all kinds of important contacts with mother has, among other things, a definite color; if it is really skin it has to possess that color! McDonald points out that the black African has as much doubt about, and defensive contempt of, white skin as the white American does about black skin. Similar defensiveness has been observed in the opposition between yellow and black, white and yellow, and so forth. An analogous principle undoubtedly applies to the ancient conflict between the Jewish and Aryan proboscis, the circumcised and uncircumcised penis, and the garlic-laden and non-garlic-laden body aroma.

The threat of black skin to a white man goes beyond the fact that it makes him aware of the potential transformations that could occur in his own body. Black conjures up bad and negative meanings. It is obvious that both in the dictionary and in common usage the word *black* is considered to be a label for that which is evil, dirty, and anti-

God. Until the attempts of the black community to make "black" beautiful (and it remains to be seen whether the effort will be successful), there was little question of its demeaning connotations. Note Kovel's (1970, p. 84) comment on this point:

> The nuclear experience of the aversive racist is a sense of disgust about the body of the black person based upon a very primitive fantasy: that it contains an essence—dirt—that smells and may rub off onto the body of the racist. Hence the need for distance and the prohibition against touching.

Goodman (1964) did, indeed, find that young children often think of Negroes as being dirty. McDonald offers a variety of examples in which white children equate black skin with dirt. She describes a white child who touches the skin of a Negro boy and says, "Dirty face." She also presents data that suggest that the "dirty" black skin is associated with feces and other unmentionable body things. Kovel (1970, p. 86) points out: "There is the coarse racist epithet 'boogie,' a word applied both to the black human being and to specimens of mucus that, because they come from the body, automatically become a symbol of dirt." Building on this concept, it has been proposed (Kovel, 1970) that the prejudice of the white against the black represents to some extent a revulsion against intimacy with that which is dirty. But going one step further, Kubie (1965) speculates that what really potentiates the negative view of black skin by the white is that he projects onto it all of the dirty and disgusting feeling he has about his own body and psychological self. In other words, as soon as a white man encounters a black man, he focuses on his black skin and associates it with the bad and the dirty, and in so doing he becomes able to load down the black man with all of his own negative self-feelings. Just as the hissing audience at a movie can transfer to the villain all of the hates and frustrations they have experienced that day, the white man can unconsciously reason: "This black skin is a badge of evil. I am so white and good by contrast. In fact, all of the defects and badness I have at times glimpsed in myself seem to go much better with black than with white. I am high and the black one is low. He is the one who really is smeared with the disgusting stuff I thought was in myself." The black scapegoat can be loaded down to relieve his white compatriot. Obviously, the same mechanism has been used to make a scapegoat of the Jew with the symbolically "dirty" nose, the bad (dirty), smelly Irishman, and many others. The black skin more easily lends itself to becoming the "dirty" target, but when circumstances require it some other body part can be symbolically suffused with dirty properties. Slanted eyes, long hair, and beards can become insignia of filth. It is apropos to add that women, who have often been treated as a minority group, have in numerous cultures become the target of the label "unclean." There are widespread customs that are based on the assumption that certain events in a woman's body make her an unclean person for varying lengths of time. Even the most discriminated against ethnic and racial groups have involved themselves heavily with this smearing tactic against women. The disgust with menstruation and the elaborate taboos about menstruating women have much in common with the behavior shown by the white man toward his black brethren.

There is indirect scientific support for the idea that the fervor of a person's hostility toward the "different" body is partially a function of how much negative self-feeling he needs to unload on that body. The more that an individual is filled with feelings and fantasies that are self-critical and self-attacking, the more important it becomes for him to find an outside fall guy. A psychologist (Rubin, 1967) looked at the changes in prejudice toward Negroes felt by white persons who participated in a group sensitivity training workshop that was designed to give insight into personal motives and to help in the understanding of aspects of self that had been kept hidden. He found that those who profited from the group experience by becoming more positive and self-accepting toward themselves also became less prejudiced toward Negroes. When negative feelings about self were replaced with more positive ones, there was less need for defensive (and self-whitewashing) tactics toward the black man.

Almost as alarming as the person with the black skin is he who is grossly aged ("dirty old man"). The stark signs of aging tell the story that the body is not immutable and that it is subject to decline. There could not be a more vivid communication about the instability of the body. So that although aging is a natural part of the life cycle and at any given time involves a large segment of the population, it is regarded as an alien phenomenon. The person of advanced years is made to feel that his body is despicable and that he is unworthy. He becomes a projective target for many of the fears and concerns of others. The younger person learns, in terms of the practices he sees supported all about him, that it is permissible to cast the aged individual in a depreciated role—to ascribe to his disturbingly deteriorated body a variety of bad things. There are real analogies between the negative language employed to describe the old person and that used by the bigot to portray minority ethnic groups. Sadly, even those who most indignantly protest that they are treated as racial inferiors adopt an equally discriminatory attitude toward their own elderly brethren. They, too, are ready to downgrade what they consider to be an inferior body model and to proclaim the superiority and greater stability of their own corporeal platforms. It is also striking that just as the Negro or Jew learns to downgrade his own body in the fashion preached by those who are alarmed by his different body, the aged person accepts his Insignia of Deterioration. Ironically, almost all persons, no matter how superior their stance has been, come to comprehend what it means to have the inferior, wrong kind of body.

One of the most frightening forms of "bad" body in our culture is that which belongs to the homosexual (particularly the male homosexual). It may even be worse to have a homosexual body than to have a black skin or a Jewish nose. The image of the homosexual body seems to be terrifying. There are young men hospitalized in psychiatric institutions who have been driven into a frenzy by the fantasy that they have homosexual attributes. The homosexual body conjures up an image of an unspeakably defective structure, one that communicates the possibility of reversing sexes. Since the sexual traits of the body are major markers in helping the individual to classify and make sense of his body world, if these markers are not secure, then he cannot have much faith in any of the conclusions he has arrived at about his body. He has to reject vehemently the kinds of body phenomena he links with a homosexual orientation.

The dread that many people feel in the presence of a body to which they ascribe bad attributes seems in part to be based on a primitive form of logic that has been well described by Frazier (1959). He cites a cluster of examples of behavior in cultures around the world in which people seem to assume that body qualities are like some elemental substance that can be passed on from one body to another by mere closeness or contact. For example, he describes an Italian belief that if menstrual clothes are put into the wash on top of, rather than underneath, a man's clothes, the man will consequently suffer intense sympathetic (menstrual-like) pain.

The association that has been suggested by Kovel (1970) and also Kubie (1965) between the black skin and dirty substances like feces is of special import because of the painful difficulty that most people in Western cultures have in reconciling themselves to their anal functions. It is impossible for a child to grow up in our society without the feeling that anal substances represent the extreme of what is disgusting. All of the messages that he gets about bowel control, performing toilet functions in private, and deodorizing the bathroom tell him that feces are the most potent form of dirt in the whole universe. The difficulty faced by the average child after he comes to this realization is that he has to cope with the fact that his body is full of this quintessence of filth and that he never ceases to produce it. This means that a lot of people feel permanently soiled. They have to devise ingenious ways to deny these feelings or to temper them. Freud has dscribed in what is probably valid detail some of the obsessive-compulsive ritualistic techniques for undoing that soiled feeling. By dint of watchful cleansing of one's body and rejection of all "dirty" thoughts, the soiled condition of the body can be refuted. There are many persons who are constantly alert and ready to project their soiled sensations onto a target like black skin, which can so easily be assigned anal qualities.

Other varieties of bad body feeling can also be projected in this fashion. People who experience their own sexual sensations as stained can slough them off onto the black epidermal target. Witness how often the stereotype of the bad Negro includes the idea that he is sexually loose and depraved. Paradoxically, this stereotype is often mixed with the idea that the bad sexuality is linked with a superior sexual potential. At the same time that the creature with the black skin is darkly inferior, it is also strangely superior and even to be envied. The white man would certainly like to have the potency that he fantasizes the Negro to possess. Some inkling of this peculiar ambivalence about the black person's body (simultaneously dirty and yet terribly powerful and potent) is provided by the fact that white people are intrigued by the possibility of darkening their own skin. Millions of dollars are spent each year in our society by white people seeking a "good tan." The irrational drive to achieve a darkened skin state is so powerful that many actually injure their skins by overexposure to the sun's rays. The darkened skin may also, as mentioned elsewhere, be partially valued because it increases the visibility, and perhaps by implication, the substantiality of the body boundary. The person with a new sun tan can suddenly see his skin in a more vivid, tangible way —more distinctly a covering and bounding surface. But beyond this, the darkened skin may signify some secret identification with the potent qualities that are ascribed to bad objects and Negroes. The Devil is feared, but his powers are coveted.

The idea that the white man's attitudes toward the black man are shaped by the bad and dirty feelings he projects onto the target provided by the black skin is increasingly supported by real scientific evidence. We have conducted some as-yet-unpublished studies in our laboratory in which we have particularly looked at the relationship between prejudice against Negroes and such variables as attitudes toward blackness and feelings about the dirtiness of one's own body. This work involved the use of objective measurement techniques. It was found that persons who are particularly concerned with matters of dirt and feelings of being unclean are the most likely to view Negroes negatively. Unfavorable feelings about the color black also turned out to be positively linked with a sense of being bodily dirty.

It is highly likely that many Negroes have as negative a concept of black as do white persons. Several studies (for example, Williams, 1964) have shown that Negroes equate black with that which is bad and dirty. They necessarily perceive their own skin as being of a color that they associate with badness, and they may, just as the white man does, project onto this black skin-target all kinds of inner feelings of unworthiness and guilt. The psychiatrist, McDonald, reported instances in which black children verbalized puzzlement and extremely negative ideas about their black skin. She even described instances in which black children would refuse to eat food with black coloring (chocolate cake, for example) because black had such negative connotations to them. The black child's rejection of his own skin was particularly sadly revealed in one exploratory study that we carried out.[1] This experiment was concerned with the possible therapeutic effects of making a child more clearly aware of the boundary regions of his body. We felt that some children were simply not fully cognizant of the protective peripheral aspects of the body wall. One of the procedures we used to intensify awareness of the body boundary involved calling the child's attention to his skin (for example, by tickling and rubbing it). Quite innocently, we included both white and black children in our study, and to our surprise we found that while the procedure seemed to increase the body security of the white children, it had the opposite impact upon the black children. When the black children were strongly confronted by the experience of their own skin, they were really disturbed by it.

The intensified effort by the black community to teach its children that "Black is beautiful" is intuitively one of the most meaningful approaches that could be undertaken to cope with the attitude of the black toward himself. The black person will necessarily have to revise his depreciated view of his own body before he can upgrade his self-regard. As long as he experiences his blackness as dirty and alien, no

---

[1] This study was done collaboratively with my wife, Rhoda L. Fisher.

amount of reassuring communications about being an equal member of the human species can be effective. As long as he lacks respect for his own body, he cannot achieve a good feeling about himself as an individual. It should be added that while a black skin represents a particularly convenient surface upon which a black person can jettison inner feelings of badness and dirtiness, there are numerous examples of instances in which other body features have provided analogous self-attacking target opportunities. The Jew has universally been assigned to dirty, lowly status, and his dirtiness has been conveniently associated with physiognomic features like his bad hooked nose or his overall Semitic appearance. His sense of feeling unclean was clearly demonstrated in a study in which I participated (Fisher and Fisher, 1960) that involved a sample of Jews living in Texas. We found that these Jews, even those who had apparently achieved well-accepted status in the community and whose families had resided in the same locale for two generations, were preoccupied with sensations of being unclean. Judges were able to pick out the Rorschach ink-blot fantasies of these people by the frequency with which they contained references to "unclean" animals like the pig and the hyena.

It is initially mystifying to be confronted by the fact that the central God figure of Western culture is someone with the body of what is usually considered to be a depreciated ethnic group. Jesus was a Jew, one of those with a "different" body. It should be remembered that he is most frequently pictured in the process of having his body mutilated by being nailed to a cross. He is not only the possessor of the depreciated Jewish body but also one whose body was destructively penetrated! However, it is an intrinsic part of the tale that Jesus later overcame what had been done to his body and returned from the tomb, once more alive. I would suggest that aside from other meanings this widely accepted belief may have, it importantly communicates the idea that the body can triumph and achieve stability. We are presented with the vision that even a mutilated Jewish body can regain its vitality. This vision may help to counteract the continuous anxiety generated in people as they encounter "different bodies" and other events that tell them that the human frame is undependable and fragile. It is noteworthy that in certain Catholic ceremonies the worshipper is even given the opportunity (via transubstantiation) to incorporate, in a symbolically literal fashion, some of the body substance of Christ. The focus upon ingesting part of Christ's body highlights the important body-image implications of the ritual. The ingestion of his body adds to the substantiality of the worshipper's body. It may be that many of the stories found in Western folklore about dwarfs and others of a similar deformed body status who are able to do powerful things and to overcome adversity serve a similar body-reassuring purpose.

A fundamental question that must be faced is whether prejudice against people with body characteristics different from our own can ever be obliterated. If there were an ideal society in which race hate were not promulgated and in which different ethnic groups had equal social and economic status, would all traces of derogation of those with dissimilar body attributes disappear? I am skeptical about it. I would suggest that as long as a person feels insecure about his own body he will be stirred to a defensive response whenever he is confronted by other bodies that, by their dissimilarity, suggest the possibility that his own body could potentially and in some strangely uncontrolled way be changed or transformed. The fear of the "different kind" of body surfaces expresses itself not only in racial attitudes, but also, as previously mentioned, in reactions to dwarfs, cripples, the dysplastic, the aged, the menstruating woman, and the maimed. Despite all the effort invested by our society in an attempt to rally sympathy for the crippled, they still elicit serious discomfort. It is well documented that the disfigured person makes others feel anxious and he becomes an object to be warded off. He is viewed as simultaneously inferior and threatening. He becomes associated with the special class of monster images that haunts each culture. Almost any kind of body deviation becomes a potential source of threat and also a focus for hostility. The male admires and yet also fears and depreciates the female body. The adult may "look down" on the smaller body of the child. The child may fearfully "look up" at the monstrously big body of the adult. The fat and the thin regard each other with mutual suspicion. It should be noted, incidentally, that there are some studies that have shown that the people who react most negatively to the crippled and handicapped are those who show unusually strong prejudice toward Negroes and Jews. Basic to all of the anxiety and hostility about body deviation is the fact that the average child growing up in our world has a tough time learning to live with his body—arriving at a fairly stable concept of how it should look and the role it should play in his life. All of the problems that he encounters in terms of assimilating the gross changes in his body size as he matures, coping with the rules about when various sphincters should be open or closed, deciphering the standards applied to the different ways in which male and female bodies should look and behave, and deciding how much of the body territory belongs to self rather than to parents, leave him with a deep sense of uncertainty about body phenomena. By the time he arrives at adulthood, he feels like a battle-scarred veteran who has survived many dangerous campaigns, and he wants to avoid situations that remind him of such past dangers or hint at analogous future ones. Until means are found to diminish appreciably the anxiety that the average individual feels about his body as he is growing up, I doubt that it will be possible to eradicate negative responses to bodies "not like mine." This, of course, includes responses to people with black skin, slant eyes, short stature, long noses, and so forth.

The almost universal alarm about body vulnerability in our milieu could not be better illustrated than by the frequency of occurrence of hypochondriacal symptoms. Every physician's waiting room has ample representation of potential patients who are convinced that they suffer from serious body maladies but who turn out, after examination, not to have any detectable pathology. They come with every form of complaint and often with the conviction that a major breakdown in some body system has occurred. Many are so imbued with a sense of body fragility that they make a career of their fancied malady. No matter how much medical reassurance they receive about their symptomatology being unfounded, they persist in their pain and discomfort. It is a measure of how troubled they are about the body that they hang on to their illusory symptoms even in the face of authoritative information to the contrary. For them the world narrows down to the body. Or one might say that their body feelings expand to fill all of the available space. Their communications are almost entirely wrapped in body metaphors. They must call attention to their bodies and at the same time announce their sense of corporeal inferiority. In a tangential, upside-down way they get a taste of what it is like to be in possession of the bad body assigned to black persons or members of other depreciated ethnic groups. The hypochondriac feels that he possesses an Inferior Body. But what is different is that he takes the initiative in publicizing this inferiority. Of course, it is possible that he is just as much victim as are black people. He may, via his hypochondriasis, be stating a sense of body depreciation that was foisted upon him by parental attitudes. It is difficult to say because our knowledge of the etiology of hypochondriacal complaints is still close to zero. What is especially puzzling about the hypochondriacal symptom is that it seems to feed reassuringly upon itself. In some skewed fashion the chance to repeat the sentiment that "There is something wrong with my body" is sought after and provides a curious form of security. There are also other kinds of maneuvers that people use that seem to be directed toward advertising that they are in possession of depreciated bodies; the possible utility of doing so will also be analyzed shortly.

It is interesting how often the negative confrontation with the "racially inferior" body "not like mine" takes the form of a fantasy in which there is close bodily intimacy. The white bigot conjures up the horrors of being married to a black person and being subjected to all of the intimacies that go with marriage. This kind of fantasy is exemplified in the now famous and corny question, "How would you like your sister to marry one?" In other words, the confrontation does not remain one of casual encounter. The "other body" has to be, at least in imagination, drawn into close proximity, touched, and somehow brought into contact with the most private areas of one's own body. This is a measure of the vivid involvement produced by the sight of the "different" body. It cannot be treated casually. It immediately stirs unescapable emotion and psychologically penetrates into the most private realms. The intensity of the psychological responses stirred by the image of the "different" body renders that body an instant, intimate associate. It represents "out there" an inner version of self that every individual has fearfully contemplated at some time or other. This may help to explain some of the elaborate schemes that are used to exclude those with a "different body" from regular societal participation. It becomes terribly important to keep them out of sight and to relieve the intense closeness to which the beholder is subjected.

Despite the anguish that goes with having body features that are "different," it is paradoxically true that many people seem impelled to advertise to others that they possess what is usually considered to be an "inferior" body. The attire of the typical hippie represents an announcement that might be paraphrased as follows: "My body is unattractive, different, deviant, dirty, ugly, and even difficult to classify sexually." Disagreement might exist about this matter, and some would argue that the hippie is simply declaring his independence of convention and his natural (non-formal) approach to his own body. While there are important elements of truth in this view, I would point out that the hippie's costume does result in his being assigned to a minority depreciated status by most other people. It does label his body as different in a way that is usually considered to be inferior and depreciated. The hippie body is perceived by most people as ugly and dirty. This, of course, is the stereotyped role allotted to most depreciated racial blocs.

There is much secret fascination in many cultures with the idea of making one's body repulsive to others. It can sometimes be seen in the play of the child who experiments with the effects of contorting his face and crossing his eyes. It is even more obvious at the time of Hallowe'en, when there is an orgy of self-distortion. Every possible way of making one's body ugly, grotesque, and frightening is used. One of the prime aims is to make one's body so grotesque that it will elicit alarm. This illuminates one of the secondary satisfactions that the individual with a "different" body may derive from his state. He becomes aware that he disturbs or disconcerts people, and while this is a matter of sadness and disappointment to him, it is also strangely ego-inflating. It represents a way of exerting control over others and is especially satisfying because the others are perceived as rejecting and cruel. The black person who discerns that his black skin is arousing alarm in someone may simultaneously feel terribly rejected and glad that he can have a disturbing impact. He also senses that although he has been rejected he has become a peculiarly intimate and close object to the person pushing him away. So, one of the attractions of making one's body look grotesque or depreciated is that it provides a means for upsetting and yet destroying the psychological distance from the detractors "out there."

The aggression that may play a role in the hippie's advertising his body in a depreciated way may also represent an elemental way of seeking freedom and expressing creativity. The urge to reshape one's body in a fashion that challenges all accepted standards may arise from the same creative charge that is found in the act of the artist who boldly tries a new form of expression. Analogously, as I suggested earlier, some of the experimenting with clothing fashions that characterizes women may be a channel for the urge to be novel and creative.

I wonder whether those who choose to dramatize their bodies in a negative fashion may not represent a vanguard response to, and an attempt to adapt to, the body-game rules laid down by the conditions of city living. Life in the city, and now increasingly even in rural areas, is built around associations with machine artifacts of various kinds and with diverse people. The machines run the gamut from giant buildings to traffic lights, vacuum cleaners, and soda-pop dispensers. There is a clear, implicit message that the human body is small, fallible, and on the way to being replaced as a source of power and strength. Further, the congested heterogeneity of the city population tells each inhabitant that his own body is only one among a huge mass (and, as such, of diminished importance as a single unit) and exposes him to the constant spectacle of bodies that are extremely unlike his own. He not only witnesses that other bodies can differ from his own in color but also spectacularly with respect to hair style, delineation of sexual attributes, and even intactness. In a large congested population an individual is likely to encounter many examples of people who are crippled or in some way seriously disabled. All of these factors must lead to an increasing sense of body uncertainty. The individual becomes less and less sure of what his body is for, how it should look, and whether it provides a stable platform for "being." Thus, when one finds that blocs of people in our culture are increasingly advertising the depreciated qualities of their bodies one cannot help but wonder whether this is not in some way a sensible adaptive maneuver. It may be a way of openly declaring what is a true state of affairs: man's body in the urban technological world has become a depreciated, alienated object. This provides an isomorphic, outside body representation of how people really feel on the inside. It formulates a threatening problem in fairly obvious body language and makes it difficult to avoid considering and worrying about. Paradoxically, the man with the black skin or the Jewish nose who has already learned some of the tricks of coping with a deviant, depreciated body may have the jump on the average city dweller who is only beginning to become aware of how uncertain is the status of his own body in the present scheme of things.

Some persons make a professional career of presenting the body in an awkward, grotesque fashion. They are the comedians and clowns. They make people laugh by portraying peculiarities and inferiorities of body appearance and movement. The comedian decks out his body and puts it into postures that look ridiculous. He builds on the depreciated state of his body to satirize and arouse amusement. It is no accident that the stock in trade of many comedians has consisted of ethnic themes, ethnic accents, and body shortcomings (stuttering, for example). They hold up to public ridicule many of the body themes that are so widely disturbing. One can, in some ways, compare the comedian with those who have "bad" and different bodies. However, there is a clear difference; he is obviously pretending. At the very moment that his body depicts the extremes of clumsiness or the grotesque, it is understood that he can reverse the whole thing and regain a state of body normality. Greenacre (1955) has proposed that writers like Swift and Carroll, whose major works derive their impact from depicting extremes in body distortion, were themselves preoccupied with feelings of body inferiority and instability. One might conjecture that analogous body concerns would be found in the comedian, the body satirist. In any case, the comedian's personal and professional motivations put him into a public role where he can act out and present for fantasy elaboration, in a safe, humorously buffered setting, the universal body anxieties. Incidentally, both Negroes and Jews have evolved elaborate "kidding" jokes about those very aspects of self that the outside world ridicules and rejects. In-group humor about "bad" ethnic qualities apparently helps to adapt to the pain of possessing such qualities.

It may be relevant to this whole matter that in times of crisis, such as in Hitler Germany, there is often a turning to mass spectacles in which great arrays of people whose bodies are all conspicuously dressed alike in uniforms are displayed. I am sure that such displays have a variety of overdetermined purposes, but one of them may be to assuage doubts about the basic stability of The Human Body. Thousands of bodies are shown that look alike and even move precisely alike to the beat of a drum. This is a dramatic way of proving that the body is a constant and well-defined thing. It is no accident that a prime theme that Hitler trumpeted again and again at such mass arrays was the fact that Germans possessed Aryan bodies and that he was going to destroy those who had tried to mongrelize these superior bodies. Similarly, the white bigot is aghast at the idea that the white body will be spoiled by interbreeding with blacks. In times of crisis there may be a need to prove that although things are tough it is still true that one can depend on the stability of one's body. The body must remain soothingly unchanging and predictable. It would be worthwhile investigating whether periods of crisis stimulate waves of uniformity in attitudes toward and presentation of the body. Are disturbing times reflected in a need to prove, in compensation, that all bodies are soundly alike, not deviant or vulnerable to unexpected variation? Perhaps the sweep of a new fashion that results in all women of a certain age category wearing a common new uniform is a direct response to forces that are so fundamentally disruptive as to require a counter demonstration that the body is still well under control.

The fury elicited in others by the deviant body is a measure of the centrality of body stability. Relatedly, it should be noted that the really vitriolic forms of verbal aggression in our culture take the form of emphasizing the deviance of someone else's body. The most superlative hostility is conveyed by pointing out how someone's body has too little or too much of some attribute. The deviant qualities that are pointed out often have to do with anal and reproductive functions.

But it is the translation of anger into body imagery that gives it the greatest negative charge. No denunciation can match using such terms as "shitty" or "bastard." When the denunciation involves both body deviance and body dirtiness it attains the acme of angry depreciation. It is just such double negativity that is ascribed to the black, the Jew, and other unacceptable minorities. They not only have "different" bodies, but also filthy ones. To accuse someone of having a dirty, deviant body is to put him in the category of those who cannot be accepted into the group because their body appearance is too upsetting to existing body concepts. There is no more insulting accusation. The use of body metaphors to dramatize anger is a fairly special case. I have not been able to think of many examples of body metaphors that comparably accentuate emotional attitudes in other categories. Even with reference to eating and loving, it is not common to depict the extremes in response by using words that particularly focus on body imagery.

What happens to the body concept of the Negro or Jew who is given the message that his body is inferior? Obviously, and as already stated, he becomes convinced that his body is substandard. This is well illustrated by a number of ingenious experiments that have been able to demonstrate that Negroes secretly feel relatively more negative toward pictures of dark-skinned than toward light-skinned Negroes and more negative toward black than toward white person representations. There are also reports in the literature in which black children show a preference for white as compared to dark-skinned dolls. But beyond this kind of negative self-appraisal, what else happens? We do not have any scientific data to answer this question, but let us scan possibilities. One thing that is probable is that a range of adaptive mechanisms comes into play to cope with the induced conviction, "I have an inferior body." Simple denial is certainly ineffective. There is no way that the individual whose body is labeled as "bad" can live in the culture and evade being bombarded by the prevailing sentiment. The intensity of the bombardment is such that it gets through any simple counter-defenses that take the form of "I don't believe it" or "It's not true." However, one related defense is to accept the idea that one's body is bad, but with the reservation that among the total of bad bodies it is still relatively superior. The light-skinned Negro can see many darker-skinned ones beneath him and be as rejecting of them as the white bigot is of him. Actually, he makes use of the same strategy as the white—projecting on to someone else's bad body certain negative and anxious feelings about his own body. Similarly, it is also well known that a defensive brand of anti-Semitism flourishes among some Jews. There is, in addition, the well-known phenomenon that Jews and Negroes may disparage each other, and so forth.

Another possible way of coping with one's bad body is to reject and minimize its very existence. This means paying slight attention to it and attaching low importance to body feelings and sensations. Life styles that focus on intellectuality and restricted use of the body imply such a strategy. There is a Jewish tradition of investment in cognition and scholarly reason that may at least in part serve as just such a means for downgrading the significance of the body. Incidentally, as previously mentioned, Kagan and Moss (1962) observed that male children who early learn to doubt the substantiality of their bodies are those most likely to become highly involved in intellectual activities later in life.

It is also not unlikely that many persons react to their bad bodies by vigorously trying to upgrade them. This upgrading process could run the gamut from plastic surgery (to remove particularly bad chunks of the anatomy) to exercise and cosmetic programs for increasing body strength and attractiveness. Further, there might be an investment or immersion in body experiences that seeks to cancel out the negativity associated with the body by proclaiming that it is aroused and important. To invest in the intense self-experiencing of one's own body is to refuse to reject it. This intense self-experiencing could derive from vigorous exercise, the use of the body for aggression, unusual amounts of eating, and so forth. It is even possible that certain drugs might be utilized to heighten body sensations as a way of asserting that "I feel my body vividly; I experience and enjoy it; the sensations that I am having are my own choice and they prove that my body is not simply a bad stereotyped thing invented by the prejudiced." Apropos of this point, it may be significant that Negroes and Jews have been strongly attracted to the use of drugs. They may find the drug experience to be a dramatic vehicle for rising above the concept of the "bad" body.

In the course of treating schizophrenic patients I have encountered a fair number of instances in which their symptoms represented a delusional acting out of the entire drama of the "bad" body. Typically, one is confronted by an individual who develops the idea that something unpleasant has occurred in his body and that this unpleasant phenomenon is offending others. For example, one man felt, quite without rational foundation, that he smelled bad and that people everywhere were avoiding him for this reason. Other patients may feel variously that a part of their anatomy is usually ugly and offensive to others, or that some past bad behavior (masturbation, for example) has been visibly imprinted on their features and consequently holds them up to public ridicule, or that they possess some body power (for example, evil eye) that injures and antagonizes others. In each of these instances the individual feels that his body is offensive to other people and that he must therefore expect to be excluded from the group. It should be added that such fantasies often occur in people who have all the outward credentials of the "good" body. They are white, not deformed, and not members of any minority ethnic group. I mention this to underscore the prevalent subterranean nature of the "bad" body probem. Under the right stress conditions, people with perfectly acceptable anatomy are delusionally drawn into the fray and publicly proclaim themselves to be what others so much fear. This is an extreme psychotic version of milder but equivalent concerns that most other people probably harbor within themselves. These milder versions can be channeled in multiple ways. One of the most direct and yet sublimated expressions that I have heard about involved a white reporter who disguised himself as a Negro and then wandered through the southern part of the United States to get the "feel" of what it was like to live among whites while occupying a discredited black body (Green, 1900). In this professional, reportorial way he was doing what others often do much more covertly and symbolically. Each person probably attempts in his own way to get the feel of the "bad" body role. When people are anxious about some problem or theme they look for opportunities to "try it on" or to rehearse it—hoping to learn ways of successfully coping with the threat involved.

It is my impression that a situation that is particularly likely to activate anxieties about having a "bad" body is that in which the individual must appear publicly before an audience. He has to stand before massed observers who have the opportunity to scrutinize him minutely without his having the opportunity to defend himself by means of counter-scrutiny. His body is the center of group focus. This is, of course, also gratifying. But we know that even highly successful public performers may be chronically plagued by intense anxiety as they prepare to step into the spotlight. Those preparing for public appearances are hypersensitive to possible deviations in their appearance. Each hair has to be precisely combed into place, every smudge removed, each article of clothing tugged into fitting "just so." There is the fundamental concern that the massed observers will come to a decision that they have before them a seriously imperfect object.

Interestingly, the anxiety of the person in the spotlight often shows itself in body terms—a sense of muscular awkwardness, sometimes blushing and other visible skin color changes, voice difficulties. Public performers not infrequently fantasize that their bodies will fail them, that they will lose their voices or be unable to move in some expected way. The shy, embarrassed adolescent who feels that all eyes are upon him as he enters the group exemplifies still another context in which an individual feels that his body is on trial and likely to evoke rejection. The embarrassed adolescent can be as negatively preoccupied with his depreciated image of his body as a Negro entering into an all-white social group.

The distress stirred up in someone who feels he has a defective body when he finds himself interacting with a person whose body he perceives as not defective (and therefore presumably superior to his) was highlighted in a study done by Comer and Piliavin (1972). They set up an experiment that hinged on the special tactics of a confederate of theirs who interviewed a series of persons with gross physical handicaps (for example, amputation, paraplegia). The confederate presented himself to half of these persons as a normal, bodily sound individual and to the other half he portrayed himself as having a crippling leg defect. In the "I am crippled" condition he conveyed this image by sitting in a wheelchair and wearing a leg brace. While he was conducting his interviews with various crippled persons, they were carefully observed through a one-way mirror by several judges who noted how often they smiled, the frequency and duration of their remarks, the amount of "eye-contact" (looking directly at the other's eyes) with the interviewer, and so forth. In other words, information was gathered that would indicate how uncomfortable they were. The results indicated that the crippled individual was less uneasy when talking with a person he thought was stuck with a defective body like his own than when he was with a person he perceived as possessing a "better" body. Those who were in the presence of the experimenters' confederate when he was presenting himself as having a "good" sound body smiled less, spoke less, were more motorically inhibited, and made less "eye-contact" than those who interacted with him when he was displaying a defective body. The individual who perceives his own body as defective experiences the presence of a sound body as a reproach to his inferior state and he becomes disturbed. As we have seen, an obverse kind of formulation is also true. He who has a sound body perceives a defective body as a threatening prognostication of what could happen to himself.

We have already discussed in several contexts the conditions of living that make people so sensitive to, and therefore defensive toward, the sight of anything that even remotely challenges the soundness and stability of the body. The natural uncertainties of biological reality are alone sufficient to create such sensitivity. When one adds to this the sum of potential violence in the world and the associated implicit message that it is easy to get hurt, there is obviously a continuous background of gross proportions to keep people on edge about the body space. But going beyond these background factors for the moment, it might be profitable to ask how parents add to the problem by their treatment of their children's bodies. There are probably body-related attitudes adopted by parents that ultimately reinforce racial prejudice. Some of these have already been discussed. We have, for example, considered the tendency of the parent to make his child feel that his body is dirty (and therefore inferior) because of the unpleasantness of coping with his anal functions.

There are two special aspects of parental behavior that I would particularly like to emphasize as probably playing a role in the widespread defensive over-response to the "different" body. One has to do with the parents' (particularly the mother's) closeness to the child's body. The child's body is regarded as a possession ("You belong to me"), and at least in the early years of the child's life there is an automatized tendency for the parent to regard anything that happens to the child's body as if it were really happening to his own. This attitude normally weakens and after a while the clearly separate nature of the child and parental bodies establishes itself. But in many families this takes a long time to happen and may not be complete even by late adolescence. What I would highlight about this state of affairs is that it gives the child an early and basic message that may be paraphrased as follows: "Your body is not a separate object. Whether you like it or not, your body is connected to mine." But hidden in this "connection" message is also the idea that the parent's body is partially a possession of the child and that what happens to the parent's body must have an impact on the child's. This might be compared to the circumstances in which Siamese twins who are joined learn that what happens to one will affect the other. In other words, the child gets a picture of the world as a place in which human bodies cannot be autonomous. The mutual "you own me and I own you" pattern that they learn in interaction with their parents later makes them feel that all relationships with other bodies potentially have some of this quality. An inappropriate sense of closeness to any other body that is encountered is encouraged. It is this inappropriate attitude that makes the white person feel so alarmed at the sight of a black skin. I would speculate that at an unconscious level the encounter with the black skin quickly triggers off the "Your body belongs to me and mine belongs to you" fantasy that was so assiduously fostered by the early relationship with the mother and father. The individual cannot look at the man with the black skin and see him as a separate entity whose blackness has nothing to do with his own body. No, he has to become involved with the implications of potential, mutually proprietary, closeness to a black body.

A second aspect of parental behavior that bears on the child's prejudice against the "different" body relates to the widespread determination to shield the child (and self) from the sight or smell of any aspect of body that is considered to be unusual or unpleasant. The modern parent makes it clear that body products are to be hidden as quickly as possible, that death and disease are too threatening to be viewed and should be banished to the funeral parlor or the hospital, that the genitals are not to be openly or calmly inspected, that menstruation or the sight of any kind of blood is shocking to behold. The child is brainwashed into feeling that there are a lot of ghastly events associated with the body that are too overwhelming to be gazed upon. The child is made to feel that he is too fragile to face up to the natural vicissitudes of the body world. So, as soon as he is confronted by a body phenomenon that is a bit out of the ordinary he feels impelled to do something defensive and self-protective. He has to get rid of the phenomenon—do something to minimize or exclude it. It is no wonder, then, that a member of the normal body majority who comes upon the sight of a discrepant minority-type body almost reflexly reacts in a defensive way.

In my zeal to introduce the concept that feelings about one's own body influence racial attitudes I may have exaggerated the importance of this factor. It is difficult to say, because the whole matter awaits more searching study. But I would like to point out how universally the sight of the "different" body arouses hostility and rejecting strategies. Across diverse cultures and economic systems racial prejudice has existed and still does. I think we will fail in our efforts to eradicate irrational racist behavior until we cope with the irrational body anxiety that feeds it.

CHAPTER FIVE

Body decoration and camouflage

When Cinderella went to the ball disguised as an elegant, high-status figure, she was really not behaving terribly differently from most people as they don their costumes each morning in preparation for their round of daily contacts. Each of us has an elaborate ritual of grooming and putting on of clothes that is intended to slant the impression we make. You can't reconstruct your body but you can, by means of clothes, exercise choice in the type of façade you attach to it. There is no doubt that we are all fascinated by the process of clothing ourselves. There are few things that involve us so continuously. In our clothing choices we reveal our values and life intentions. Anatole France wrote:

> If I were allowed to choose from the pile of books which will be published one hundred years after my death, do you know what I would take? I would simply take a fashion magazine so that I could see how women dress one century from my departure. And these rags would tell me more about the humanity of the future than all the philosophers, novelists, prophets, and scholars. (Rudofsky, 1947, pp. 17–18.)

As we decorate and clothe ourselves, we are, in a sense, doing a self-portrait. The layers of camouflage that we apply are intended to

85

fill out an image that we have in mind. By the time we are adults we have had a chance to experiment with many different façades or "fronts." We have learned to dramatize certain aspects of our appearance and conceal others. Our use of clothes might fancifully be compared to that of camouflage experts who have been given the job of concealing certain facts from observation—and perhaps even creating a few illusory ones. Actually, it is an oversimplification to imply that there are only one or two major factors that determine how a person chooses to dress. Even aside from the fact that you may want to look a certain way, your clothing choices could be influenced by economic considerations or fashion standards. Because of limited income you may have to buy cheap clothes that create a special image by virtue of their cheapness (Roach and Eicher, 1965). Or you may fit yourself into the latest fashion costume because you want to conform, in spite of the fact that this costume is discrepant with how you want people to see you. But I would add that factors like wealth and socioeconomic status were once of much greater importance in determining how a person dresses than they are today. As mass production of quality clothing has progressed, persons of low income can look quite well dressed. It is more and more difficult to identify a person's social class from his clothes. Also, the range of competing fashions on the current scene makes it less likely that anyone will get locked into a style of attire that is grossly different from his true preference. There is plenty of opportunity in Western culture for each individual to put on his camouflage according to his own unique wants.

Several investigators have tried to understand the major motives that enter into clothing choices. If you question women about their choices they specify a number of different intents. Some say they are primarily interested in wearing things that are "comfortable"—not restraining, inhibiting, or difficult to put on. Others indicate that they want clothes that make them look attractive and elicit admiration from men. Still others emphasize winning social approval or being conservatively modest or creating an aesthetic impression. Whatever the general definition each individual gives about why he dresses as he does, I would speculate that his overall purpose is to tell himself and others that he is a certain kind of person. One researcher has shown that women and men differ in their basic dressing motivations. Women seem to be more concerned with winning approval with their clothing strategies. Men were found to be largely interested in avoiding disapproval of the way they clothe themselves. The majority just want to get by without their clothes drawing criticism. Of course, more recent developments suggest a growing inclination for young men and women to dress in a way that will not avoid but rather provoke disapproval by the Establishment at the same time that they are looking for approval from their peers. Clothes have taken on new importance as a way of protesting and expressing opposition. There are many precedents for the use of clothes to convey political and ideological messages. The black shirts of the Fascists and the robes of the Ku Klux Klan are examples.

It is interesting, also, to note that the absence of clothes—nudity —has often been used as a weapon of protest. There are religious sects that have dramatized their opposition to particular laws by parading naked in the streets. Nudity is also a popular means for adolescents in Western societies to demonstrate their contempt for the constraints of the Establishment. Some schizophrenics announce their withdrawal from what they consider to be an unbearable world by dramatically throwing off their clothes and running out into the street. The implications of nudity as a way of declaring one's complete freedom have often elicited strong countermeasures from those in authority. Nudity is punishable by death in some cultures. The Roman Catholic church has taught in convent schools that it is sinful to expose your body even to your own eyes. The wearing of clothes represents a form of submission to prevailing mores. It is like putting on a "citizen's uniform" and agreeing to play the game.

Nudity may be used in a magical way to negate the world as it is. It may be used as a way of declaring that one wants to see a major change in nature. It can become a vehicle for asserting that all of the usual rules are cancelled and that a dramatic new state of affairs prevails. There are nudity ceremonies that illustrate this point. In one culture the women strip themselves naked at times of drought as part of a plea for rain. In another a woman whose child is seriously ill removes all of her clothing and goes to the goddess's temple at night as a way of appealing for help. An Eskimo feels that he must strip naked when he eats venison and walrus on the same day—otherwise he will cause serious pain for the soul of the walrus. There is implicit in such behavior the idea that a violent change in the state of one's body may help to instigate or cushion the effect of what is considered to be a radical state of affairs in nature. Goffman (1963) has noted that body exposure may be used as a way of expressing trust or security. He points out that a woman may wear a dress at a ceremonial ball that reveals much more of her body than she allows to be seen in everyday circumstances. He goes on to say that this may be a declaration on her part that she feels so secure in that social circle and trustful of the good conduct of its members that she can expose herself without fear of being exploited. It is well known that strong elements of temptation and counterbalanced control are built into the framework of the conventional nudist camp. Puritanical codes of male-female interaction often prevail. The exposure of the nude body, with the obvious sexual temptations involved, is carefully balanced by a network of restraining rules of conduct.

One study (Roach and Eicher, 1965) found that when people are asked to think back on their early clothing experiences, images of coercion pop up. They remember that they were made to wear this or that article of clothing. Or they remember that they could not wait until they were old enough to choose their own clothes. Clothes are frequently associated with being controlled and regulated. It is mother who is almost always recalled as the person who dictated how one would dress. She was the "instrument of coercion." The researchers who gathered this information wondered about the feminizing effect of the fact that the boy's appearance was controlled by a woman. They suggest that because mother manages the appearance of her son, via her clothing selections, for so many crucial years he probably has to cope with an image of himself that contains many feminine elements. He is stuck with an early image of himself that has been shaped by the standards of a woman. For some men it may take a great deal of undoing, for example in the form of wearing extremely "masculine" clothes, to cancel out the image that Mom cherished.

What do we really know about the impact of clothing? If I dress in a certain fashion, will this perceptibly influence the way others evaluate me? Attempts have been made to explore these questions. In one experiment audiences were asked to give their impressions of people who posed in different types of clothing. In another, raters evaluated people who were represented only by pictures of their heads and then again when they were depicted full-length in various costumes. Evidence has emerged from such studies that clothes do, indeed, affect the impression you make on others. But the strength of the effect depends upon how well-known you are to them. If another person is not personally acquainted with you, he is more likely to let his opinion of you be influenced by the character of your clothes than if you are well-known to him. It is when you are the anonymous stranger that people are especially dependent upon the appearance of your clothes to cue them about what sort of person you are. Those who are close personal friends are only slightly affected in their opinions of each other by the clothes they happen to wear on any one particular occasion. This suggests, of course, that those who have intimate, long-term relationships, like husbands and wives, are somewhat immune to being influenced by each other's costume changes.

To what extent is a person's feeling about himself influenced by what he wears? Since we are all presumably well acquainted with ourselves one might not expect much change in self-feelings as the result of clothing change. But the analogy may not be reasonable. After all, when we change clothing it is the appearance of our own body that we alter, and in that sense we are much more ego-involved with the alteration than with one we perceive in another person. Furthermore, costume shifts may actually involve tactual and kinesthetic shifts that are not apparent to the outside observer. One set of clothes may feel smoother or rougher than another. One set of clothes may be experienced as tighter or looser than another and therefore affect how free or inhibited we feel. It is also possible that each of us has learned through long trial and error that putting on certain clothes does affect our mood or level of anxiety. Perhaps specific clothes duplicate specific childhood experiences or help to defend against particular forms of uncertainty. It will be recalled that one experimenter found that schizophrenic women may choose clothes with loud patterns as a way of making their body boundaries more visible and therefore more psychologically substantial. Some people might find that the caressing smoothness of a costume reinstates pleasurable contacts with mother's body remembered from early life. A bright, cheerful outfit might serve as a repeated reminder to oneself that life need not be sad or bad. In other words, it is possible that the clothing we wear delivers more powerful messages to ourselves than it does to others.

A person may choose a style of dress because it helps him to control his own conduct. This is obviously true in religious circles. To cover the body fully and to conceal its sexual qualities may "help" the individual to avoid the temptations of the flesh. Hasidic Jews believe strongly in the power of clothes to regulate behavior. They wear distinctive costumes that set them off from surrounding communities and that also identify the strata within their own ranks. Those who are most religiously devoted wear such articles as a black, large-brimmed hat, a long black coat, and white knee socks. The members of the sect feel that by wearing distinctive garb they are helped to avoid sin. One is quoted (Poll, 1962) as saying: "With my appearance I cannot attend a theater or movie or any other places where a religious Jew is not supposed to go. Thus, my beard and my sidelocks and my

Hasidic clothing serve as a guard and a shield from sin and obscenity." Within the Hasidic community the greater the religious devotion of any member the greater the number of special garments he may wear as a badge of his virtue. But once a member begins to wear the garments symbolizing his higher status, he has to show religious behavior consistent with it. He has to keep justifying his superior garments by the frequency and intensity of his religious acts (which are carefully monitored by those who know him). In a sense we all use clothing in a manner analogous to the Hasidic Jew. We put on costumes that remind us that we are supposed to behave in certain ways in certain situations. The man who dons his expensive business suit and goes off to the office is partially cueing himself about the role he is about to fill. The act of putting on the suit and the feel of it on his body tell him that he is supposed to display certain patterns of behavior. When the judge wraps himself in his robes he is reminded that he represents the law. He knows that he is framed by his garments and that people expect him to fit his actions to that frame. The pressure of a tie that is correctly tight may be a persistent reminder to someone at a formal affair that he has to be on his best behavior. The release from the constriction of the tie may help to arouse images of taking it easy and doing as he pleases. Paradoxically, the person who cultivates an appearance of uncontrolled disarray confines himself to the expectation that he creates in both himself and others that he will behave unconventionally. He defines his intent by his clothes and he would feel that he had failed unless he publicly fulfilled this intent.

The actor represents the extreme case in which a person's role is defined by his costume. When he puts on certain garments he becomes one person, and with another set of garments he is a new character. His façade bears much of the burden of defining who he is and of projecting a convincing image of that identity. The actor must learn to change his style of behavior to fit his latest disguise. There are those who have said that the actor has a tough problem in maintaining a stable concept of who he is because he is so often trying to fulfill the demands of his latest costume. The question arises whether, in a more attenuated form, any individual may build up sensations of insecurity about self-definition if he is called upon to do a lot of shifting from one form of costume to another. Does the woman who, in her effort to stay in fashion, changes from one extreme of dress style to another feel a bit hazy about herself for a while after each change? We do know that some people suffer rather severe disturbance to their identities when they suddenly switch from their usual civilian garb to army uniforms or prison outfits. I recall, too, the distress of a group of men we studied when they were suddenly and unexpectedly confronted in the mirror by masks we asked them to wear that depicted feminine rather than masculine features. Does it jar the policeman to spend part of his day in a uniform and the rest of the time in civilian clothes? There is a good deal that we need to learn about such phenomena.

Definition of self through clothing is expressed at another level in the popular custom of tattooing. Millions of people have had words, designs, and pictures permanently engraved on their skin. These engravings may at times cover a large area of the body. They are like a second skin or a colorful, close-fitting garment. They are analogous to the popular sweaters that feature words, phrases, and pictures; they advertise your alignment with some sentiment or idea. Tattoos have been found to be a way for adolescents in prisons to declare their solidarity with each other (Burma, 1959). In one school for male delinquents about 67 percent of the inmates were observed to have tattoos; in a similar school for girls the total was 33 percent. Those who were tattooed averaged from five to ten different kinds over their bodies. Most were in clearly visible locales, and interestingly a greater proportion were visible on the girls than on the boys. The words and phrases in tattoos frequently indicated identification with a gang or an expression of alliance with an important figure (like a mother or a significant friend). When questioned, the delinquents seemed to be somewhat aware that their tattoos served to advertise their affiliations with power sources. It is a way of declaring: "I am such and such kind of a person and you can expect me to behave in certain brave, strong, forceful ways." It is interesting that tattooing is found in about 10 percent of the population of the United States, that it is much more common in men than women, and that it seems to increase in frequency during periods of crisis.

The significance of clothes in defining what you want to be could not be clearer than in the case of the transvestite who dresses up like a woman. Although he is anatomically a man, he announces his intention to fill the role of a woman by disguising himself in a woman's garments. In so doing he is not only telling others that he wants to be a feminine object but he is also addressing himself. Once having taken the step of putting on a feminine façade he can act out other aspects of a feminine way of life. His feminine fantasies become real, and in his new disguise he can test out what it feels like to be perceived as a woman. He can also test out how it feels to perceive himself as a woman. Although the use of a feminine masquerade by the male occurs again and again, it is fairly rare for a woman to try to pass herself off as a man. This is remarkable in view of the fact that in our culture the female has more liberty to experiment with the garments of the opposite sex than does the male. One might think that if women had more opportunity than men to try on the male façade they would also more often be tempted to adopt it, but such is not the case. Perhaps the fact that male clothes have not been forbidden to them makes the donning of such clothes less of a dramatic, magical gesture. The male who has been deathly afraid of touching his body with female garments may be drawn to them as we are to all things that are terribly forbidden. The act of putting on women's clothes would for a man represent a venture into something extremely mysterious and out of the ordinary. As such, it lends itself to the expression of the dramatic urge to change identity.

Incidentally, it has been observed that in childhood girls feel freer to try on their mothers' clothes than boys do their fathers' garments. This is but another example of a tradition that makes it more acceptable for the female than for the male to experiment with changing the appearance of the body. The feminine flexibility about clothes is simply a special case of a general freedom to shape and reshape one's body with plastic freedom. There is one area in which men have had more freedom than women in decking themselves out: they have had more uniforms with official significance available to them. For a long time men, but not women, were able to qualify for a great variety of official uniforms (for example, police, army, fireman's, train conductor's). But it is interesting that even in these instances each uniform carried with it a detailed definition of role that was really quite rigid and restricting. In other words, uniforms probably did not provide men with the same freedom to alter self-definition as did the range of costumes in a woman's repertoire.

Costumes are also used in an attempt to control nature. It has already been mentioned that in several cultures people try magically to change natural events by displaying their nudity in a ceremonial way. The stripping off of their clothes is a novel act that is supposed to set in motion a corresponding novelty or change in the way things are unfolding. People wear amulets and good-luck charms in hope that the attachment of a potent object to the body will shield them from the dangers in the world. The costumes of priests presumably give them a special "in" with the great forces of the universe. Relatedly, some cultures believe that if a person wears the clothes of another who has been successful it will endow him with similar success. One investigator (Gillin, 1951) reported that when he was living with an Indian group there was a surprising demand for his old cast-off clothes. He notes (p. 39):

> In my own case at the close of each season I gave away several garments to what I believed to be deserving cases. At first I thought the great avidity with which they were begged for was based entirely on utilitarian motives, but I discovered later that some of the recipients of these felt they would keep with them a certain part of my essence by having my clothes. One man to whom I had given a pair of trousers in 1942 had a long story of his adventures to tell me in 1948 in which he attributed a large part of his good luck to his trousers. He kept them carefully in a box and wore them only on important occasions or times of crisis.

The magical and irrational use of clothes to control nature pops up even in our own scientific milieu. It was once the custom to carefully isolate patients hospitalized for the treatment of tuberculosis. The personnel who cared for them were expected to wear special protective masks and other clothing to shield themselves against contagion. But observers in one tuberculosis hospital found that the higher the status of a particular member of the hospital staff the less likely he was to wear the protective clothing when he approached a patient. Physicians often failed to don protective masks whereas ward attendants almost always did. Even more strikingly, it was found that hospital personnel who carefully wore protective clothing when near the patient in a professional capacity would not wear such clothing when talking to him in an informal social setting (for example, at a movie). What this adds up to is that the protective clothes were officially assigned to personnel in a ritualistic way, as if they would help them to avoid being infected, but this was magically ceremonial. In actuality, there was an unstated feeling that the clothes probably did little good.

The basic style of dress in any culture partially recollects the attitudes that culture has historically taken toward the body. Quite a number of standard decorative details in clothes represent traces of past customs. The cuffs on men's trousers, the nick on men's suit collars that divides the collars from the lapels, the differential right-left placement of buttons on women's, as compared to men's, garments —all represent survivals of past clothing styles that are no longer functional but have stayed on out of inertia and also as a symbolic bridge to the past. When one looks at the clothing configurations of Western society, certain obvious and yet provocative facts emerge:

1. They have assigned considerable significance to distinguishing between the sexes. The distinction has primarily involved the difference between the trouser, which encloses the lower part of the body, and the dress, which leaves the lower body sector open.

2. Usually, they have required that the body be completely covered (except for the hands and head) and, in addition, have called for more than one layer of clothing.

3. Generally, they have called for points of constriction or careful fastening. The neck and the waist have been favorite sites for applying constricting pressures.

4. They dictate that the color and design schemes of garments will have a certain minimum harmony or relation.

5. They usually avoid gross right-left asymmetries. The right side usually looks exactly like the left, although recent styles have experimented more with right-left differences. Upper-lower asymmetries are considerably more common.

6. Directly or indirectly, they have typically been designed to draw the eyes of the beholder to body areas with sexual significance. This is done either by exaggerating the size of the area or by concealing it in an overdetermined manner.

7. They have, with rare exceptions, built in definitions of worth or status in terms of the quality or financial worth of the garment.

8. They seek to distinguish age levels (although this is less and less true).

Some of the fundamental values of Western society with respect to the body are obviously reflected in these clothing patterns. The fact that we so carefully assign different clothes to the two sexes reflects our chronic anxiety about matters of sexual identity—whether one's body is unequivocally in the right sexual category. The closed versus open attributes of the garments covering the lower part of the body in men and women probably also reflect a strong need to make it clear that the male body is not penetrable whereas that of the female is. It is pertinent to this same issue that right-left clothing asymmetries are usually avoided. There are research findings (Fisher, 1970) that indicate that the right-left gradients of the body are symbolically associated with splits in the sexual identity of the body (for example, "Am I partially masculine and partially feminine?"). To emphasize differences between right and left may symbolically dramatize the possibility of conflict about the sexual classification of one's body and therefore stir uncomfortable anxiety. On the other hand, it is interesting that clothing contrasts between the upper and lower body sectors are quite common and really encouraged. This may express a message that we learn from early childhood. We are made aware that the lower part of the body, in which the anal and sexual functions reside, is bad and the upper part good (cleaner). This is probably one of the most fundamental distinctions inculcated in our society. Toilet functions are dirty and should be hidden. The clean and the filthy should be separated. Our clothing strategies seem to duplicate this distinction. The use of belts to divide upper and lower, the piling on of layers of cloth to conceal the lower sections, and the definition of upper and lower as different by means of the use of contrasting colors —all may contribute to the segregation of bad lower from good upper. But, interestingly, the very overdetermined way in which it is done often only calls attention to how concerned and preoccupied people are with the whole theme. This is, of course, also true with respect to the simultaneous highlighting and coy concealment of sexual areas by means of clothing. Our ambivalent preoccupation with sexuality is of amazing intensity, and there is little question that the concept of the body as a sexual instrument has emerged as a dominant motif of our time.

The concern about proper matching of design and color in one's clothing, which was mentioned above, may have important aesthetic roots, but it probably also derives from the need to experience one's body as properly integrated—all the parts working together. It is further true that the individual is constantly searching for ways to unite his body with his life role. He wants his body to mirror, and to be sensibly related to, what he has achieved in life. It is no wonder, then, that people try endlessly to cloak themselves in impressive clothing. The person who is proud of his social attainment (for example, as the result of accumulating wealth or power) tries to impart these same qualities to his body by covering it with "rich," high-status garments.

The analysis I have just attempted is simplistic and only skims the surface. There must be much more about the history of our body values that serious analysis will be able to derive from the nature of our clothing practices.

What do we know about the personalities of people who wear different types of clothing? There are all sorts of stereotyped ideas about what you can judge to be true of a person from his clothing. For example, those who wear dark conservative clothing are supposed to be conservative and well controlled. Those who wear sexy-looking clothes are supposed to be sexy. Those who wear bright colors have been said to be emotionally expressive, and so forth. Few of such formulations have been scientifically tested, and we do not know how valid they are. One difficulty that I see with most of them is that they are too simplistic. They assume that a person's traits are directly and visibly transmuted into his style of behavior. But the process is much more complex. People may express a trait in one area of behavior but not in another. Or they may defensively express the opposite of how they really feel. Someone who is chronically a bit depressed may try to fight this feeling by wearing bright colors; it would be wide of the mark in his case to assume that his bright attire meant he was cheerful and light-hearted. In a study carried out in my laboratory we found that you could not distinguish sexually responsive women from the non-sexually responsive on the basis of their appearance or clothing. We asked judges to pick out from a series of women's pictures those who were most sexually active and arousable. The sexual attitudes and behavior of these women had been thoroughly studied. There was only a chance relationship between the judges' evaluations of sexiness and what was actually true of the women. The sexual responsiveness of a woman could not be determined from how colorful or feminine or frilly or revealing her clothes were.

In fact, as you scan the published research concerned with whether people who wear certain styles of clothes have specified personality traits, the yield is sparse. Several attempts have been made to show that secure and insecure people differ in how they dress, but no consistent results have emerged. The dimension of dominance-submission has also been studied. But there is no convincing evidence that dominant people dress in an obviously different fashion from submissive people. It has been demonstrated (Roach and Eicher, 1965) that people with high self-esteem say that they are less concerned about whether their clothes are modest and socially acceptable than are those with low self-esteem. There is an interesting trend (Roach and Eicher, 1965) for persons in the higher socioeconomic classes to be more aware of clothing cues and differences than are those in lower classes. In the higher classes there was a greater tendency to draw conclusions about others on the basis of their attire. Relatedly, another study (Bethke, 1968) detected a tendency for Anglo-American women in Texas to be more sensitive to clothing differences than Mexican-American women living in Texas. These findings suggest that those who are of relatively dominant social status and who would presumably have more resources to spend on clothes, are especially likely to use clothing cues in making judgments about others. Is this a form of snobbery? Those with superior clothing resources can afford to use clothing criteria to classify others on an inferior-superior continuum. Note, by the way, that the middle classes seem to be most responsive to the successive waves of new clothing fashions. In contrast to the upper and lower classes, they are the ones who shift most radically from very short to very long and back again to very short skirts, and so forth (Roach and Eicher, 1965).

A surprising result has been reported by Compton (1962). She could detect no relationship between a woman's clothing preferences and her actual physical attributes. Preferences were not correlated with eye color, hair color, height, and weight. At a more psychological level, Compton did find that women who prefer small rather than large designs in their dress fabrics are particularly feminine and interested in making a good impression on others. She also found that those who prefer deep shades and saturated colors in their dresses are more sociable and less submissive than those who reject such shades and colors.

Attempts to find consistent changes in clothing preferences with age have not been very successful. A few trends have been spotted. For example, there is a decreasing preference for bright, saturated colors with increasing age. But the findings are really minor in character. Differences between the sexes during the developing years resolve themselves primarily to the fact that girls are more conscious of and interested in clothes than boys. Girls also seem to exceed boys in the extent to which they perceive clothes as a way of establishing that they are mature and grownup. Girls regard the putting on of makeup and certain articles of clothes (the brassiere, for example) as definite badges of their grownup status. But age differentiations in clothing styles for men have all but disappeared, and this is an interesting phenomenon in itself. At one time, the male went through definite clothing stages—for example, from short to long pants—in the process of growing up. However, it is now accepted practice for little boys to wear long pants. Of course, it is generally true that the male makes use of a much smaller range of clothes than the female and is also less likely to wear special garments to match specific social occasions.

Women certainly do attach great importance to clothes as a method for enhancing sexual attractiveness. Many styles have been designed to magnify the pelvic sector and to highlight symbolically the sexual reproductive functions of the feminine body. Crawley (1931) points out how broad, flowing skirts accentuate the pelvic shape and maternal functions. He refers to the "crinoline or farthingale" as the "culmination of the distinctive feminine garment." He adds that the adoption of the corset and related garments not only narrowed the waist but, by contrast, enhanced the abdominal and gluteal regions. Also, by pushing the breasts upward, it made them more prominent. In fact, the tight, corset-like garment further enhanced the breasts by displacing the breathing direction of the lungs upward and imparting breathing movements to the mammillary region. It is obvious, as one surveys the patterns of various cultures, that there are remarkably different ideas about what makes a woman's body sexually attractive. What looks like mutilation or shapeless obesity to one group is a powerful aphrodisiac to another. What one group uncovers for effect, another covers. We are told of one group, the Naga, in which the women cover their breasts but not their genitals. They are quoted as saying (Crawley, 1931): "It is absurd to cover those parts of the body which everyone has been able to see from their birth, but that it is different with the breasts, which appear later."

All of a woman's body-grooming and decorating is not sexual in its intent. In fact, it may paradoxically be a way of controlling the impact of her sexuality. It may be used to conceal and control rather than to excite. Wax (1957) points out, for example, that women who work in an office where there is close association with men in a small physical space may need to neutralize their biological attributes and make it clear they are there in a non-sexual capacity. They may use cosmetics and clothes to minimize natural shape, to obscure all trace of body odor, and to tame the undulation of body movement. In short, they seek to convert themselves into impersonal surfaces. Or a woman may seek through her attire and grooming to establish the fact—only tangentially sexually related—that she is not old or deteriorating. She will conceal body areas that reveal her aging and expose those that are most youthful. While maintaining her sexual desirability is part of this strategy, it is secondary to proving that she is not an old woman.

One observer feels that even when women dress to look sexy, their behavior should be regarded as only a special case of their desire to be appropriately sociable. They want to be identified as feminine by virtue of their interest in being sexually appealing. This observer (Wax, 1957) adds (p. 593) with astute thoughtfulness:

> A woman grooms herself to appear as a desirable sexual object, not necessarily as an attainable one. In grooming herself, she is preparing to play the part of the beauty, not the part of the erotically passionate woman. In this sense, cosmetics and grooming serve to transmute the

attraction between the sexes from a raw physical relationship into a civilized *game*.

The fascination of women with clothing may represent, in part, the fact that it has provided one of their few means for advertising status. Until fairly recently, women were relatively blocked in their attempts to achieve outside of the conventional housewife-mother role. A man who has been successful in his work and who has risen in the world gets a lot of approving feedback from his work associates. He also can tell people that he has such and such an important position or role title. His wife does not have these means of getting recognition, but she can proclaim her own sense of importance by the cut and value of her clothes. Her garments function in the same way as the uniform of an army officer of high rank; the splendor of her grooming announces that she should be accorded a salute. In this context, one might predict that as women find more diverse ways of getting public recognition they will have less need to win the sort of general, anonymous approval they get by means of splendid clothes. It is pertinent to this point that studies have found that several minority groups of low status in our culture that seldom win personal success spend an unusually high percentage of their income on clothes—in an apparently compensatory attempt to advertise themselves and to elicit admiration. Some schizophrenic patients I have known, in a bizarre caricature of such compensation, would concoct weird costumes for themselves that were guaranteed to draw attention wherever they went. But on the more positive side, and also as an illustration of the ego-saving function of compensatory clothes practices, I would cite several published accounts of how institutionalized schizophrenic women have been helped in their recovery by being provided with clothes and grooming advice that markedly bettered their appearance. Let me add, as an aside, that it may be true that women who are forced to become inmates in institutions (for example, prisons, mental hospitals) that put everyone in standard uniforms and interfere with usual grooming strategies suffer more than men in equivalent places of confinement. It may be more important to a woman than to a man that she be able to maintain the special cosmetic façade that she has worked out for herself. A man's sense of identity may be less dependent upon maintaining his usual outer appearance.

Goffman (1963), a sociologist, has pondered the many ways in which grooming is used to maintain propriety. Clothes and grooming serve as a way of telling others that you are disciplined and have adequate self-control. Clean hands, carefully combed hair, shined shoes, properly buttoned up garments—all give the message of a careful and sustained interest in one's own appearance. This, in turn, signifies mature and responsible intent. The self-control conveyed by the way we wear our clothes is part of a total picture, which includes posture. The proper woman not only dresses in certain ways but is careful to keep her knees together when she sits down. She must not reveal any of her thigh or her underclothes. Goffman points out that one becomes aware of how much restraint the average woman imposes on her appearance after one visits a psychiatric ward in which schizophrenic women live. In this situation women sit with their thighs exposed, scratch their genitals, leave garments unbuttoned, and so forth. It is a bit startling to become aware of just how hard most of us work to maintain an acceptable "controlled" public image. Goffman notes, in the same context, how concerned the average man is that he not expose his crotch area publicly in an unseemly way. He may check his fly zipper before entering a group and when sitting may use various techniques for covering up his genital region. The power of clothes to dictate proper behavior is brought home by the fact that a woman who has just come from the beach where she wore a bathing suit covering only a small part of her anatomy will become embarrassed if her skirt shifts to reveal briefly her upper thigh. When you wear a bathing suit it is okay to show most of your anatomy publicly. When you wear a conventional dress, it is a sign of moral looseness to let anyone look beyond certain body boundary lines. An entertainer who has just revealed her body to an audience in her scanty costume may be embarrassed if she unexpectedly reveals too much leg as she gets into her car after the performance is over and she has shifted to street clothes.

A peculiar form of behavior vis-à-vis clothing is seen in the fetishist. He is one (almost invariably male) who cannot obtain gratification from the sex act unless he is looking at or touching some special object. He has to have ritualistic contact with some thing, which rarely has any prominent sexual significance itself, in order to enjoy sexual interaction with a woman. He is, in a sense, like the child who cannot go to sleep unless he can clutch his favorite teddy bear. Frequently chosen fetish objects are shoes, corsets, feet, and various clothing articles made of leather or rubber. The fetishist may be able to attain orgasm simply from a brief period of closeness to such objects. In its extreme form, the fetish demonstrates the fact that an article of clothes can take on a powerful, symbolic meaning. Even within the normal range it is obvious that certain feminine articles of clothes can by themselves evoke strong sexual arousal in men. The average man finds the sight of feminine underwear exciting. But what distinguishes the fetishist is that he *cannot* become sexually aroused unless a certain article is present on the scene. Psychoanalysts have suggested that the presence of the fetish provides some form of reassurance to counteract an anxiety that interferes with sexual arousal. They speculate that the anxiety specifically has to do with the realization that the female does not possess a penis and therefore that a man could end up without one, too. The fetish is presumably an extra something that reassures the man that he need not be concerned about losing anything in the course of his sexual encounter. It should be repeated that this re-assurance is like that which a child gets from his teddy bear when his mother says goodnight and leaves his room. In attenuated form we probably all use clothes in fetish-like ways. We all have favorite out-fits that make us feel more comfortable or more self-assured or more something. It is common for a person to have a special hat or pair of shoes that he feels brings him luck. Some people do not feel at ease until they have buckled on a certain belt or put on a particular piece of jewelry. There are women who have a sense of anxiety and incom-pleteness until they put on a brassiere. There are males who feel in-complete until they have put on a sweater or a ring with a potent, engraved insignia. In other words, articles of clothing not infrequently serve as substitute teddy bears.

The conclusion is inescapable that clothing has numerous ag-gressive connotations. The protective use of clothes to do such things as keep out the cold and prevent skin damage is essentially one of warding off unfriendly natural forces. Obviously, too, there are forms of clothing that have been designed to make the wearer safe in the midst of aggression. Armor and bullet-proof vests are good illustra-tions. Clothes have on many occasions been used to scare, intimidate, and demonstrate authority over others. Dracula's cape and the soldier's uniform have a good deal in common. It is significant how uniforms and related kinds of outfits are utilized to mark large numbers of people as potential sources of aggression and therefore as warnings to the enemy to keep his distance. The uniform of the soldier designates stored aggression that can be tapped when necessary. Someone has jokingly said that uniforms do more to make war feasible than any other invention. Without uniforms it would be difficult to distinguish one side from another and perhaps also difficult to get large numbers of people to fight in unison. The rich and the privileged have long used clothes to announce their superiority and to keep underlings in their place. There are kings who proclaimed in no uncertain terms that particular modes of dress could be legally worn only by people who were officially considered to be noble. For example, silk and velvet could be donned only by members of the upper echelon. The act of wearing such materials indicated your belief that you were of greater rank than those not permitted to wear them. The superior one tries to degrade others by the insistent visibility of his special garb. A survey carried out by one investigator revealed that a prime thing that concerns people buying new clothes is whether these clothes will adequately impress others. There is a basic need to use clothes to make a forceful or controlling impact on others. This is an aggressive perspective. The readiness of people to link clothes behavior with aggression is illustrated by the quickness with which an individual can stir up hostility toward himself if he appears publicly in an inappropriate costume. One is reminded that the coloration and appearance of birds and animals serve, among other things, to transmit warning signals to others.

More needs to be said about the use of clothes to muffle the body. It is possible to cover your frame with layers of cloth that render your body almost invisible to yourself. The average middle-class man wears a costume during working hours that conceals every inch of his skin except for his hands and head. He cannot with ease directly touch the major parts of his trunk. His skin sensations result primarily from the pressure and movement of his clothes, and there is not too much of that. Since his clothes also help to maintain rather constant temperatures, he has few temperature sensations. It is true that he can quite directly experience the sensations from the interior of his body, but even they seem distant, as if they were being picked up through the thicknesses of enfolding cloth. The feet, in their heavy leather casings, are well insulated from the ground and there are only the dull pressure variations that accompany each successive step. Even the eyes are increasingly screened from direct contact with the world by glasses of various kinds. The impact of the sun on the eyes is muted by dark filters. In fact, such filters are being used more and more to attenuate the sensory impact of ordinary indoor illumination. What all of this adds up to is an attempt to reduce the possibility of variation in body experience. It is a way of declaring that it is unpleasant to have to cope with unexpected changes in patterns of body sensation. The avoidance of such changes may be comfortable but it removes some of the adventure of relating to your own body. One might say that it results in boredom with one's body. Nothing ever happens.

There are isolated high points that accompany eating, sexual arousal, and a few other regulated body functions, but the flow of body experience is otherwise flat. One cannot help but wonder whether some of the semi-desperate body things that people do are attempts to relieve corporeal flatness. Great orgies of eating, seeking sexual contact in psychedelic circumstances, massively arousing physiological systems with drugs or alcohol—all may be efforts to break through the regulated body boredom both symbolized and actually implemented by clothing. It is interesting that some cultures (for example, the Russian) have emphasized the control of the young child by swaddling him in a thick wrapping that is both insulating and confining. This procedure seems, among other things, to reduce the extremeness of emotional response. Do we, in a sense, chronically swaddle our adult bodies with some of the costumes that we have adopted?

The self-mothering that lies behind many cosmetic and clothing practices is rather intriguing. It is considered immature for an adult to be too solicitous toward himself. You are not supposed to baby yourself or take tender attitudes toward your own person. A child can, without loss of face, kiss a part of his own body or openly undertake a major maternal-like rescue of a sector of his skin that has sustained a small contusion. An adult who was equally open would be ridiculed; however, under the guise of self-grooming and dressing attractively an adult can do a lot of babying of his own body. It is considered acceptable for someone to spend long periods of time rubbing and caressing his own skin if it is done in the name of rubbing in oil to combat dry skin. Relatedly, one commentator has pointed out that in the name of applying sun-tan lotion it has become acceptable for couples to rub and caress 95 percent of each other's bodies publicly. There is no end to the opportunities for self-nurturing in the self-grooming process. A woman can scan and pat her own face with fervent tenderness as she fixes her eyebrows and puts on various layers of makeup. She can try on dresses by the hour as she solicitously seeks garments that fit her just right. She can dust herself with baby powder and do so with the full support of advertisements that affirm that what is good for baby is good for you. Even the process of getting a sun tan, which is regarded as an important aspect of looking attractive, permits long periods of passive snuggling with the warmth playing on your skin. The maternal care implicit in self-grooming is especially revealed in the increasing tendency to tie good appearance to eating properly. People can focus great concern on whether they are eating just the right amount of food, getting enough vitamins, and so forth

—all within the province of achieving attractiveness. Of course, we all half realize the narcissism in our grooming binges. We can certainly spot it expertly in others. The self-babying in the behavior of someone else who spends inordinate time or money in body grooming soon becomes obvious. But we are likely to miss its full implications in ourselves. It would be interesting to know whether self-grooming increases in times of deprivation or crisis. Does a person mother his own body more when he feels alone or in unfriendly territory? The amazing effectiveness of the advertisers in getting people to buy an exotic array of body-grooming products may reflect the fact that these products allow people to nurture themselves gracefully. They provide one of the few acceptable opportunities to lavish love on your own body. It is possible that those who are most devoted to self-grooming are those who are generally most in search of love and affection. I suggest this on the basis of a study I conducted (Fisher, 1972) in which it was found that the greater the amount of energy married women expend on grooming and dressing, the higher are their intercourse rates. I interpreted this finding, in the context of others that also appeared, to mean that self-grooming and a high level of sexual activity were manifestations of a broader desire to be narcissistically gratified.

Clothes serve us all when we need to disguise ourselves. The bank robber who wears a mask to hide his identity is only acting out in extreme form what is a popular practice everywhere. We all use clothes to conceal things. We obviously hide our nakedness, we keep our body defects out of sight, and we put a veneer over the signs of our aging. But, in addition, I think we use clothes to conceal what we regard as badness within ourselves. We may even wear garments that are designed to trick others into believing that we are the virtuous opposite of some brand of disrepute. The girl who is tempted by bad sexual fantasies that frighten her may eventually choose to conceal her sense of corruption by covering herself with a nun's uniform. The man who is ashamed of his urges to do immoral and illicit things may choose to fasten on the badge of the policeman. There are probably many complex ways in which we manipulate our outer appearances in order to hide inner feelings that shame us. One person may do so by simply concealing or obscuring himself. He may wear a beard, mustache, sun glasses, and bulky enfolding clothes—all of which act like a mask to ward off scrutiny. If people can't really see you they can't tell how you feel inside. Another may adopt the strategy of putting on such an anonymous, nondescript appearance that he is psychologically invisible and therefore not likely to be scrutinized. I have also been struck by the way in which some people can dress themselves to represent *one* very forceful impression or image and do so in such an overpowering fashion that the question of whether there is anything different underneath would not be raised. The clothes of a man may declare with unchallengeable intensity, "I am a conservative, successful, and obviously admirable person." Those of a woman may declare, "I am a very beautiful and desirable creature and you need know nothing else about me." Relatedly, some women make themselves psychologically invisible by always wearing the exact uniform dictated by the latest fashion. In this way they are perceived in a stereotyped, conventionalized way that discourages looking at the real person who is acting like a clothes mannequin. I wonder whether parents do not use the bodies of their children as auxiliary façades to counter things in themselves that are unacceptable. An angry mother may dress her daughter to look angelic as a way of denying her own disquieting dissatisfaction. Or she may dress her children splendidly and herself neutrally so that all potentially probing eyes will be upon them rather than upon her. Other concealing practices may involve calling attention to a particular part of one's body as a way of denying "bad" urges linked with another part. For example, a woman may use all of her skill to call attention to her face as a way of distracting the gaze of others from her "bad" pelvic area, which she equates with unacceptable sexual fantasies. A woman with a deep sense of inferiority about her intelligence may highlight her legs as a means of calling attention away from her head, which she associates with the intellect. I would suggest that nudity is so embarrassing to most people not merely because it uncovers the genital areas but also because it removes layers of covering that help to conceal inner feelings. It is not mere coincidence that people often loosen their clothes or peel off a few layers of their decorative façade when they prepare to express strong emotions in an open, frank manner.

I have picked up cues in some of my clinical work that the woman who is unusually beautiful and who often finds admiring eyes upon her may develop the feeling that what is inside her cannot live up to the outer façade. She is gratified by the admiration she receives but wonders whether her beauty is deceptive. She asks herself whether people would admire her if they knew more about what was beneath the surface. She may even defensively become angry over the fact that people are drawn only to her superficial beauty. It is, in fact, difficult for the stuff she sees inside herself to match the brilliance of her outer aspect. She knows that people will not admire her inner self as much as they do her surface beauty. This disparity may leave her with a sense of being counterfeit. The problems of the beautiful woman are also complicated by the fact that she usually arouses a good deal of envy in other women, even her own mother. She may, therefore, from an early age see reflected back in the faces of other females feelings of hostility and reproach that undermine her inner self-concept. I know of instances in which extremely beautiful women have, as a result, developed the irrational feeling that they are unattractive and even ugly. One investigator (Burian, 1970) has shown rather amazingly in his study of a group of married women that the greater the degree to which their bodies conformed to the cultural ideal-body physique, the less satisfied they felt with their sex-role functions, their view of themselves, and their bodies! It was also true that they were less likely to be rated as satisfied with their marital-interpersonal relationships by their own husbands!

The issue of attractiveness versus ugliness plagues most people. There is widespread concern about being ugly and a lot of dressing-up is concerned with defending against such feelings. The problem has been exacerbated by the fact that we are constantly reminded by the communications media that a truly attractive person looks like such and such a movie star. We are all presented with idealized images of what is attractive and are given the message that they are far above us. Few women can match the glory of the carefully cultivated image of the movie queen that appears on the screen. They cannot escape a sense of disparity and ultimately of inferiority. Some of the new clothing styles that dramatize being unattractive and unconcerned with appearance are obviously a revolt against the unfair tyranny of Hollywood standards of how an acceptable human being should look. It has not been sufficiently advertised that almost anyone can be beautiful to someone else. A recent study (Cross and Cross, 1971) found that when pictures of a range of people were shown to others and judgments were obtained about their attractiveness there was not a single one that did not receive at least a few positive votes. Even the least popular of the pictured persons was seen as very attractive by a few of the judges.

CHAPTER
SIX

Lilliputians and giants:
expanding and contracting body

One of my favorite pictures portrays a small child looking painfully and awkwardly up at an adult who towers over him. For effect, the artist partially disconnected the child's head from the neck and tilted it at an impossible angle. I can remember once getting into a similar posture when I twisted my head to get a clear view of an enormously tall skyscraper. It is an uncomfortable position and gives some hint of the problems that a small child has in adapting to the bigness of the adults with whom he lives. Jonathan Swift, in relating the story of Gullivor's visit to the land of the giants (Brobdingnag), conveys in his own exaggerated way the problems of the very small when they are in contact with the very big. Gulliver is constantly worried about getting hurt ("stepped on"). He is afraid of the great anatomical proportions of the giants, but also reacts to them with disgust. Their gross size seems inappropriate and vulgar. Even the "largeness" of their smell offends him. He is amazed at the volume of their urination. The sight of the great nipple of one of the women shocks him. The huge pores of the skin of the giants seem outlandish. In the presence of the big ones he feels weak and inferior. When he finally escapes from

Brobdingnag he finds it difficult to adjust to the small size of ordinary humans. Upon returning to his wife and children he at first believes they have been starved because they look so strangely small.

Several of Freud's key ideas about personality development were tied in with the child's reaction to discovering that parts of his body differ radically in size from those of others. He dramatized the young boy's amazement at discovering that his father's penis is so much larger than his own. Presumably, this induces in the boy feelings of organ inferiority, and, within Freud's view that a boy necessarily gets involved in a competitive Oedipal struggle with his father, serves to reinforce the fantasy that Dad might castrate him if he were too provoked. Similarly, the young girl was depicted by Freud as suffering humiliation and a sense of loss when she discovers that the boy's penis is so much bigger than her clitoris. The shocked reactions that Freud links with the perception of disparities in organ size sound a good deal like those of Gulliver as he got to know the giants.

We all start out as Lilliputians and go through the successive transformations that finally make us the giants to the next round of children. We have to master the sensations of smallness and bigness, and, perhaps more importantly, those having to do with the fact that for a long time the only certainty is that your body will keep changing in magnitude. Even when we finally settle into being of adult size we have a lot of experiences involving apparent shifts in body size. We fill up with food and water and then expel material. This evokes parallel sensations of our bulk growing and shrinking. Many other life circumstances produce contrasting size experiences. We put on "big" uniforms or costumes and also strip ourselves down to skin size; we sidle into telephone booths and then enter the vast entryways of Goliath-like buildings; we lie spread out in bed and shift to compactly absorbing the impact of acceleration in a fast car; we look up at a great building that seems immensely bigger than us and subsequently fly over it and discover that it is only of toylike dimensions. We learn to cope with these size changes and to maintain a reasonably stable image of how much space we occupy. It is amazing how well we do this considering the extremes of size alteration to which we are subjected.

Situations do arise in which people lose their ability to perceive their own size realistically. It then becomes apparent that the potentiality exists in all of us to distort our size dimensions. I have already mentioned a disturbed patient whom I was treating psychotherapeutically whose acute breakdown was preceded by the sensation that his body was somehow larger in relation to the size of ordinary doorways than it had been. There is an interesting case cited in the psychiatric literature of a schizophrenic man whose disturbance was initially registered in the sensation that his head had become too large for his hat. Persons with migraine headaches not infrequently report sensations of almost bizarre alteration in head size. Note the following descriptions (Lippman, 1952): "I experienced the sensation that my head had grown to tremendous proportions and was so light that it floated up to the ceiling, although I was sure it was still attached to my neck. I used to try to hold it down with my hands" (pp. 348–49).

Persons who take LSD get caught up with the feeling that parts of the body have become elongated or spread out. Sensations of change in the size of extremities like the hands are common. One group of investigators (Liebert, Werner, and Wapner, 1958) have shown in an empirical study that LSD produces a sense of increase in size. They had normal persons estimate their head sizes both before and after they had taken a dose of LSD. They found a significant increase in such estimates under the impact of the LSD. It is interesting that such an increase did not occur for estimates of the size of non-body objects like a dollar bill or a pack of cigarettes. The LSD size-alteration effects were specific for the individual's perception of his own body. In another experiment these same investigators showed that after schizophrenics ingested LSD their arms seemed to feel longer than they had before coming under its influence.

The hypnotic state is also one in which feelings of body-size change have been noted. During hypnosis many persons get sensations of swelling and shrinking, especially in the face and extremities. They may perceive their legs as becoming elongated. One individual reported that his legs seemed to extend from one corner of a room all the way over to the opposite corner. There are also descriptions of swelling of the head, and one person said his lips seemed so swollen that he could not bring himself to speak intelligibly. Controlled studies in my laboratory of the hypnotic condition have shown convincingly that it is normal for those undergoing hypnosis (particularly men) to feel as if they were overall larger.

What would happen to your view of your body size if you were completely isolated and did not have the usual chance to make day-by-day comparisons between your own body and those of others? Two researchers (Reitman and Cleveland, 1964) put people into a state of sensory isolation and compared the body-size judgments they gave before and afterwards. (Sensory isolation is a condition in which the individual is deprived of as much input from the environment as possible; he is blindfolded, sound is blocked out, and even kinesthetic sensations are modulated.) It was found that under such conditions your perception of your body size becomes unstable. You may see your body as either increased or decreased in extent. Another investigator, who immersed himself nude in a tank of water where he received almost no stimulation, also reported sudden fluctuations in his sense of size. This is further evidence of our great potential for losing realistic awareness of our body proportions. A fairly dramatic example of an unrealistic alteration in body-size perception is provided by the normal sequence of what happens when someone has an arm or leg (or any projecting body part) amputated. As previously mentioned, the amputated part continues, with few exceptions, to be experienced as if it were still connected intact to the body. But what is of special interest is that it gradually begins to feel as if it were contracting and growing smaller and in the final phases of its disappearance actually seems to shrink into the stump and to be residing there. This shrinking of the phantom is a vivid experience, and amputees are quite capable of drawing series of pictures in which they illustrate the process. A major illusory change occurs in a body part that has only illusory existence!

Aside from the size transformations that occur in the unusual states associated with schizophrenia or LSD or body injury, there are some that evolve in the course of everyday living. They are not as extreme but they are there to be observed. For example, it has been pointed out that in the process of falling asleep or waking up the individual may have the sensation of expanding or contracting. As you slip off to sleep, your body may seem to spread out and lose its limits—somehow diffusing to encompass a wider area. When you awaken in the morning the process may reverse itself. Suddenly you contract and you experience yourself as living in a narrower chunk of space.

In taking off and putting on clothes and shoes it is not uncommon to feel one's body become larger or smaller. When clothes are put on they tend to articulate the boundary of the body and this may result in a sense of being smaller. It has actually been shown in the laboratory that if you make a person more aware of the periphery of his head by touching it he will judge his head size to be smaller than when his head is not being touched in this way. The touching renders the outside of the head more palpable and so it feels less spread out. Obviously, many people wear girdles and tight belts because, aside from any real reduction in body volume that they produce, they also give rise to a sense of being compact, squeezed in, and smaller. It is true that the putting on of clothes can also make you feel larger. When bulky garments are added to your body they can balloon your apparent size even beyond the literal increase that results from the thickness of the garments themselves. A large pair of overshoes can transform your feet into giant appendages. Some people choose clothes and hair styles that will make them look big, and they get a sense of security out of this augmentation. The expanding versus reducing effects of clothes probably interact, and each individual learns from experience what kinds of clothing will give him the body size he most prefers. I would add that the wearing of a uniform that advertises authority or prowess may enhance a person's bigness. The policeman who puts on his uniform or the general who dons his regalia probably feels literally larger as a result. I would assume that the same is true for the expensive business suit of the executive and the uniform of the athlete. Increasing numbers of women are donning uniforms, too (as members of police forces, for example), and I would presume that they also are "enlarged" by the experience. This may trouble them because the present female ideal is smaller rather than larger.

We have all had the experience of feeling altered in body size as the result of interacting with someone who has unusual body dimensions or special significance to us. If you stand next to a very short person you will feel particularly tall, and in the presence of another who is of extreme height you suddenly become conscious of your smallness. Very thin people may give you the feeling that you are awfully wide, and a chubby person may feel amazingly thin in the presence of another who is grossly obese. There are actual experiments in which it has been shown that the person who is very tall or short does over- or underestimate the sizes of others in relation to himself. What is especially striking is that your stature may seem to shift because of the psychological impression that someone makes on you. In the presence of your boss or anyone else of great authority you may literally feel smaller than usual. One study showed that when students in a nursing school were asked to estimate the heights of a number of persons, the degree to which they overestimated was positively correlated with the amount of authority such persons had in the nursing school structure. The greater the authority of each person, the more he was viewed as being larger than he actually was. In all likelihood, this was a reflection of the fact that the nursing students felt relatively smaller as they compared themselves to figures of increasing authority. We all know that there are people who make us feel small. Someone who is critical or depreciating can cut you down. The cutting down is not merely metaphorical. If you were to examine your body feelings while you were being depreciated you would discover that you literally feel reduced in size. There is a clever experiment in the literature that documents this point. Students were asked to estimate their height both before and after taking an examination. One segment were told that they had failed the examination and another that they had done well. Those who thought they had failed perceived themselves as shorter in their post-examination height judgments. This was not true of those who were told they had done well. Those with a sense of having done poorly registered their impression in body shrinkage. Relatedly, let me point out that people who have prominent symptoms of depression and unworthiness are likely to portray themselves as small. It is also apropos to add that I have found in my work that schizophrenics are unusually likely to report the sensation that parts of their body seem to be smaller than they should be. I have suggested that these shrinkage feelings reflect the defeated and depreciated self-perception that characterizes so many in this diagnostic category. Overall, a good deal of evidence is at hand that feelings of psychological smallness are replicated in seeing oneself as physically dwarfed.

As was suggested earlier inanimate things, too, can register their size or authority upon people and affect size experiences. Obviously, a huge, Godlike, vaulted church can make you feel diminutive. The same can be said for a skyscraper or an immense stadium. Working in the shadow of a huge machine can probably convince you that you are a runt. A man with a shovel who toils day after day next to a great crane or steam shovel cannot but feel physically diminished. Apropos of these speculations, a study was done in a psychological laboratory in which individuals were asked to spend some time in a miniature house with miniature furniture. It turned out that this experience made them feel significantly larger. At another level, I would suppose that people who sit inside giant machines and operate them begin to expand psychologically and to feel a bigness that they suck out of their mechanical partners. I would guess that even driving an impressive big car may enhance the apparent volume of the man behind the steering wheel. Living in a house that is substantial but not of overshadowing dimensions might have the same enhancing effect. The fact that you can get a feeling of increased size out of identifying with a tool or a mechanical object was demonstrated in an experiment in which each person was asked to estimate the length of his arm when he was holding and when he was not holding a pointer in his hand. The "attachment" of the pointer to the hand made it feel bigger. One can understand the attraction of carrying a cane, a swagger stick, or a club as a way of bolstering one's sense of size. Similarly, the long train on a dress, long flowing hair, or a heavy dangling necklace might help to enhance the size of those women who, for their own reasons, feel they need such enhancement. People obviously labor to build up the size of specific body parts whose psychological importance requires a parallel size emphasis. The padded bra and the padded shoulders of the suit coat are efforts in this direction.

The presence of great and Godlike figures makes mortals feel small. In the past, during an average person's lifetime there were only a limited number of occasions on which he was likely to find himself confronted by such august personages. But this has changed radically. The Greats and the Superstars of our world are almost constantly present in clearly visible form and there is no escaping the fact that they tower over us all. Consider the giant Hollywood images that loom over us on the screens of thousands of movie houses. The face alone of the Superstar is bigger than the entire body of the individual viewer in the audience. Similar Gargantuan figures challenge us on billboards and other kinds of tricky signs. Repetition may dampen the impact of any one of the big representations, but it may in its incessant rhythm gradually convince us that we are of pretty puny proportions. How can any man compete in size with an image of John Wayne that fills the entire wall of a large building? Some of the colossal religious constructions of the past, such as the Sphinx or Buddha figures, clearly convey an understanding that the way to make the individual worshipper feel properly tiny is to put him in a position where he has to face up to the fact that he is unbelievably smaller than the Big One. Many of the ceremonial costumes used in religious rites similarly aim to impress the viewer with the great size of those who are part of the Big One's inner circle. There is, of course, the other side of the coin to consider, namely, that to be close to a Big One is to share in some of his stature. While the sheer giant qualities of a God-figure may create feelings of being small in someone during a ceremony, it is possible that a sense of being allied with such a figure may help to sustain one's sense of stature at later times. It is also possible that a person's sense of size may be bolstered by being a citizen of a large rather than a small country or an inhabitant of a large rather than a small city. It is important to emphasize again that in my use of the words *small* and *large* I am not speaking metaphorically. I think there is good experimental evidence that the individual literally alters his concept of how big he is as different positive and negative things impinge upon him. While we use a joking figure of speech when we say that someone has developed a "swelled head" because of his success, I would seriously suspect that the individual in question actually perceives his head as larger. In other words, feelings about self are translated into certain ways of perceiving one's body. This gets into the basic question of how body feelings mirror our attitudes toward events. I have proposed elsewhere (Fisher, 1970) that because your body is psychologically closer to you (being indistinguishable from your identity or existence) than any other object it serves as a unique screen upon which you project your concerns and wishes. This relationship might be compared to that of two Siamese twins who are so alike they cannot be distinguished. They act as if they are one, and each sees in the other a large segment of himself. Similarly, the cognitive, observing part of each individual feels duplicated by the body in which it is housed and attributes to it qualities that reflect its central concerns. In this way, a person who feels cut down and psychologically small in the face of someone's criticisms ascribes the same sense of smallness to his body. But this may be a circular process. Once an individual's body feels smaller, this may in turn reinforce his feelings of psychological smallness, and so forth.

When you focus on a body part because you expect to use it to accomplish some purpose, you tend to magnify its apparent size. One investigator had persons estimate the length of their arms when they were being used to point to a particular thing and also when they were simply extended without purpose. He found that the arm was judged to be longer when engaged in a purposeful act. This suggests that you will magnify the size of body parts that you consider to be especially important or useful to you. Perhaps the intellectual has an exaggerated idea about the size of his head. The orchestral conductor may experience his arms as longer than they really are. The high jumper may be deceived about the true dimensions of his legs. Of course, it is also true that the more you use a body part and directly visualize it the less likely you are to have unrealistic ideas about it. Concealed parts of the body are likely to be quite susceptible to size distortion. It is well known that men often entertain unrealistic images about penis size. Women similarly harbor distorted images of vaginal size. Several studies have shown that people have highly inaccurate concepts of the actual size of their stomachs and hearts.

If a body part fails to live up to a person's image of how large it should be, this can become a focus of chronic anxiety. The woman with small breasts may forever doubt her own femininity, even after she has married and found herself to be sexually responsive and completely fertile. So important is it, as conveyed by cultural norms, that certain parts must look the proper size! The same absurdities are encountered with reference to penis size. Men will judge the masculinity and potency of other men by penis size, and a highly potent man with a small penis may not be able to neutralize his skepticism about his own masculinity. It is a fact that we have rather strict definitions of what are proper body dimensions. Anyone who is in the slightest degree dysplastic in size proportions is viewed as peculiar—and ultimately viewed with distrust. A man whose head is slightly "too large" or a woman who is "too tall" may find themselves living in a semi-alienated fashion. Plastic surgeons are, of course, kept constantly busy trimming body parts to fit culturally acceptable size molds. Noses are shortened, breasts are enlarged, and so forth. In some cultures conformance to proper size standards requires a good deal of pain and endurance. It may be necessary to increase the size of one's lips manifold times or to submit to the cutting down of the clitoris. Of course, our size standards that have to do with obesity and being fat probably mobilize as much defensive energy from the population as any other single activity. If all the energy that goes into dieting and oral self restraint could be converted into kilowatts there would be no need for atomic reactors. It is interesting to watch how changing women's fashions dictate that first one body part and then another should be augmented or diminished. Today the breasts are to be prominent (big), and tomorrow it is the length of the leg. Cosmetic styles may dictate that the eyes are big one season and the mouth the next. Similarly, the "bigness" of head and facial hair may fluctuate dramatically for men.

It would be fair to say that in our culture the concept of body size is more closely tied in with matters of weight and obesity than with any other theme. The principal way in which an adult can change his actual size is by accumulating or losing fat. Quite radical shifts in body bulk become possible in this manner. While only a small percentage of persons experience really gross revolutionary alterations in their adipose deposits, the possibility casts a pall of anxiety over Western society. Great numbers of persons track their weight, ounce by ounce, over each twenty-four hours. They quickly become alarmed at the slightest sign of an upward trend in their weight curves. This alarm is often out of all proportion to the actual increase that has occurred. Fat is "bad" and the reaction to adding fat is as intense as that of a sinner who has violated a cardinal commandment. Up to a point it is an unstated judgment that goodness and virtue are proportionate to how free one is of adipose bulges. Even moderate degrees of obesity are perceived as disfiguring. It should be added that this negative attitude toward fat does not exist in all cultures. There are places where the accumulation of tissue is associated with respectability and even with beauty. We lack sound information as to why being fat has such threatening connotations. Negative attitudes toward the obese develop early in childhood. Studies have shown that children as young as five or six already strongly reject the obese image. One could argue that fatness has such negative meaning because it is associated with susceptibility to such illnesses as coronary disease. But this is doubtful when you consider that the negative connotations of obesity were widely prevalent before it was ever scientifically linked with illness. No, the explanation must lie elsewhere. Perhaps the test of possessing a streamlined, clearly efficient contour has to be passed by any object that can move in space before we can feel positively toward it. Or perhaps we associate fatness with being greedy and passionately narcissistic. Or it could be that in a time of great confusion about the body it is too suggestive of potential body instability to be confronted by corpulence, which dramatizes the possibility that one can, simply by eating, radically revise one's corporeal base of operations. It will be a while yet before we can decide on a valid explanation.

Many attempts have been made to understand why some individuals need to pile great mounds of fat upon themselves. There have also been investigations of the rarer cases who starve themselves down to skeleton narrowness. I will not review the network of literature dealing with these matters. Let me simply note that it has been variously theorized that obesity is due to unconscious oral wishes that have been unsatisfied, immature and regressive aims, the desire to avoid adult responsibility (including mature sexuality), and so forth.

I would like to focus on the body-image implications of radical shifts toward fatness or thinness, although this can only be done by extrapolating from the limited facts we have.

Earlier, I mentioned an obese psychiatric patient who, in the course of his psychotherapy sessions, revealed the fantasy that his fat served as armor-plating to protect him against attack. As he put on layers of adipose tissue, he felt that he was building up an enclosure around himself. It was like wearing a bulletproof vest. In the same spirit, he reacted to his growing bulk with the feeling that he was getting tremendously large, bigger than other people. He interpreted his bigness as a sign of power and a way of impressing others that he was formidable. I would suggest that this may be a fairly common unconscious motivation for eating one's way to bigness. It is interesting, in this respect, that when obese persons who are dieting lose weight they underestimate the actual decline in their bulk. Their concept of their reduction in size as the result of the weight loss lags behind the real state of affairs. The protective function of a fat sheath is pointed up by a study of obese persons who lost considerable weight while dieting. It was found that as they shed pounds their unconscious concern about being vulnerable increased. They felt as if they were more open and undefended.

There is a syndrome, called anorexia nervosa, in which persons cut their food intake so radically that they are soon reduced to starvation thinness and may actually die for lack of nourishment. This syndrome typically occurs in adolescent girls who are strikingly immature and who simply do not want to grow up. To be emaciated and gaunt is a way of remaining small and also of blotting out the incipient shapeliness that accompanies breast and pelvic development. The desire is to remain a child and to avoid the responsibilities of sexual involvement. In other words, extreme loss of weight in these girls may be directed at reducing the power of their appearance—the opposite of the desire for bigness linked with obesity.

Of course, the protection and power that an obese person may unconsciously expect from his fat represent a primitive line of thinking. It is based on childish analogies between size and power. In actual fact, the very obese usually find that their body appearances reduce their effectiveness in dealing with others. They learn that they are perceived as ugly, misshapen, and unworthy. Their status declines rather than increases. The difference between their primitive expectations and the way in which obesity is regarded in the culture must leave them feeling chronically puzzled and disappointed.

One interesting fact that has been emerging from research into obesity is that the fat person seems to be less accurate than others in judging how much he has put into his stomach. If you introduce measured amounts of material into his stomach he makes more errors than others in estimating these amounts. Even further, the obese person is more likely than others to look for cues outside of his body to tell him when it is time to eat. He is more dependent on outside rules and definitions as to when he *should* eat. For example, it has been found that on the Jewish New Year, when it is expected that persons will fast for a certain length of time, the obese have relatively less difficulty in not eating. They look to the external religious injunction as a guide to whether it is time to eat. The non-obese are more likely to tune in on their own stomach contractions to decide whether to put food into themselves. In other words, it sounds as if the obese have a defect in body perception; they seem not to be knowledgeable about how to interpret certain very important body sensations. Apparently, they have a childish orientation toward body events. They not only misperceive what is going on inside their bodies but also make unrealistic assumptions about how their body attributes will affect or impress others. This raises the question of whether they were brought up by parents who failed to give them responsibility for mastering their own body experiences. It sounds as if the parents took over the task of judging what the child's body experiences meant. They, and not he, decided whether he was hungry enough to eat. In other words, they acted as if they owned his body. Several cases have come to my attention in which very obese children were practically fused to their parents. They were not allowed to react straightforwardly to their own body sensations, but rather had to experience them through the intervening screen of their parents' interpretations. I would like to add that it was my impression that the parents would not permit these children to view their own obesity realistically or to lose weight. They devised a thousand ways to interfere with attempts to diet. They would prepare rich foods, issue messages that it was dangerous to deny food to yourself, and so forth. It is my hunch that these parents also managed to deliver oversimplified notions about size being equivalent to power. Perhaps such parents frequently express verbal approval through phrases like "That's a Big Boy" or "Show me you're a Big Boy and drink all your milk." Or they may repeatedly express admiration for anything that is large. The worship of size is at a fever pitch in Western society; a young child may absorb this worshipping attitude and literally apply it to his own body before he is able to make sensible discriminations between his body and what goes on "out there." The equation that children are likely to make between size and importance has been nicely illustrated in studies showing that the greater the money value assigned to coin shaped forms in a laboratory setting the larger they are estimated to be in size. If something is worth a lot it has to be big.

Another idea worth considering is that the parents of the obese are people who are impressed with the fragility of the body and need to have tangible evidence of its reserves and resistance to being depleted. The parent who is afraid that the body can be easily "used up" may feel comfortable only when he sees the body of his child clothed in an ample reserve of fat. He could, of course, easily insinuate this same attitude into the child, who would then be comfortable only when he felt he had an adequate treasury of fat. This kind of attitude might be fairly sensible under primitive conditions in which food is lacking for long periods of time, but it makes little sense when transplanted to a country full of supermarkets.

One of the most dramatic of all body size changes occurs in the pregnant woman. There are few, if any, comparative instances in which the body is so grossly ballooned in such a short time period. But studies of pregnant women (Fisher, 1972) indicate that, by and large, they adapt quickly to their size transformation. They do not often develop a sense of serious body distortion. I have appraised body feelings and attitudes in a large sample of pregnant women and have not been able to find a single dimension in which they differ noticeably from the non-pregnant. Apparently, if a change in body size occurs, no matter how extreme it may be, that is part of a normal, socially acceptable role, it does not arouse serious body anxiety. In fact, people seem to tolerate rather well any revision of the body if it is done within the framework of social approval. Various cultures have done such things as cripple the feet of women, remove the clitoris, and cut out or build up chunks of the face, and these practices have not only been tolerated but eagerly sought after.

Tallness and non-obese bigness suggest masculinity. All other things being equal, the larger man is viewed as more manly. There is even evidence suggesting that the larger parts of the body are seen as more masculine than the smaller ones (Fisher, 1970). We know that tall men tend to get better paying jobs than do short men, presumably because they make a more forceful impression. It has been said that the short man feels inferior and is sometimes driven to do big, masculine things in order to prove his true size. Napoleon's press to conquer Europe has popularly been explained in terms of this formula. I carried out one study (Fisher, 1964) that explored how men appraise their own height. The question was whether there are personal differences between those who have an exaggerated sense of their own height and those who underestimate it. A number of men were asked to estimate their height, and then it was actually measured. The extent to which they over- or underestimated was correlated with a number of personality measures that had been obtained. It was found that the more a man had the need to exaggerate his height the more devoted he was to proving he was a go-getter, a dominant and achieving person. But even more strongly, he was committed to the idea that the male is superior to the female. The man who has to feel bigger than he really is seems to do so, at least partially, out of a desire to prove to himself that he is psychologically bigger than other people. He is particularly interested in leaving no doubt that he towers over women. This drive for superiority easily lends itself to a compensatory interpretation. It is not difficult to reason that the man who puts himself on stilts feels that he is too small and is doing his best to camouflage his predicament.

The concept of size superiority is tied in with the notion of upright posture. By standing up man has attained greater vertical magnitude than almost any other animal. It is interesting that in ceremonial settings where there is concern about advertising the importance of some person or theme emphasis is placed upon the participants standing stiffly erect. A line of soldiers fixed at attention with their bodies thrust as high as possible exemplifies such a ceremony. We urge our children to stand up straight and regard a slouch as terribly wrong. It is as if the slouch were interpreted as an attempt to avoid achieving one's full stature and therefore an abdication of an important divine right. The strong message that we give to our children and to ourselves to walk tall may have a variety of negative effects. It has been pointed out that the "thrust up" body demands a rather stiff muscular orientation. You have to hold your muscles almost as if you were at attention in a military formation. In so doing you may stress certain focal points (for example, the lower back) and even adopt a chronic shallow mode of breathing. A sense of stiffness, which may be generally inhibiting, is introduced into the feel of the body. It is almost as if one had clamped a fixed mold around one's frame—all in the name of a special brand of superiority. We are less likely to expect exaggerated uprightness from the female than the male. She is not under the same social pressure to keep her spine stiff, and it is possible that some of the differences between male and female body concepts may derive from this fact. We know that women tend to be more comfortable with their body experiences than men, and this may be directly due to their lesser obligation to maintain a basically self-inhibiting body stance.

Let me add that some people may, in their own special ways, adopt body postures that dramatize an image of smallness. They may, because of parental attitudes or the inferior role assigned to them by society, feel obligated to identify with a "bent-over" position. They may stoop, carry themselves in a "contracted" manner, and in general convey the impression that they are about to fall into a prostrate condition. The stooped position of the man who feels he has failed or is disillusioned is classical in dramas. The anxious adolescent who stoops over because he has not yet come to terms with the implications of his tall stature is a common sight. It is my impression, too, that the aged are inclined to droop over into smallness to a degree that goes beyond the frailty associated with their age.

Women do not want to be big. They try to conform to the diminutive stereotype. They learn early in life that the ideal feminine body does not create an impression of bigness. One study (Katcher and Levin, 1955) was able to show that girls are aware of the association between femininity and smallness as early as age three. It is also interesting that in this same study there was evidence that girls arrive at a clear concept of the link between sex identity and size at an earlier age than boys do. In some ways, the prevailing cultural norms probably make it more difficult for a woman to accept the idea that she ought to be small than for a man to go along with the idea that he should be big. So much emphasis is placed on the virtue of anything that is large-scale that a woman has to work hard conceptually to discern why the same principle should not apply to her body. In fact, I wonder whether some of the specific kinds of bigness that have become fashionable for women, such as protruding breasts and high heels, may not represent a way of saying, "Yes, I am small in most ways. But I can also be big in other ways. I have the capability of bigness and therefore I am not a complete deviant from the size-worshipping standards of our time."

More should be said concerning the possible role of early childhood experiences in creating anxiety about smallness. In his first few years of life the child has the same relationship to adults that Gulliver had to the giant Brobdingnagians. The seven-pound infant may be outweighed twenty-fold by each of his parents. We do not know how this tremendous disparity registers and how much of a trace it leaves. But even by age three or four, when the child is capable of clear registration of his interactions with others, he is still many times smaller than adults and there is little doubt that he must be intensely impressed by his own relative smallness. It is not uncommon for the child's concern in this area to be expressed in all kinds of wishful references to himself as big. The child makes statements like "I am a big boy" or "Look how tall I am." He becomes offended if someone openly refers to him as "little." It should be remembered, too, that most of the inanimate objects the child encounters are built to the scale of adults and so they only serve to magnify how tiny he is. If adults had to sit repeatedly in chairs much too large for them or ride in vehicles obviously constructed for a giant species, they would get a taste of what the small child encounters. It is difficult to find out what fantasies are aroused in the child by the presence of others who tower so high over him. But some of these fantasies are probably represented in the pervasive stories and myths involving encounters between giants and their little opponents. "Jack and the Bean Stalk" is a good example of such an encounter. You may recall the explicit and implicit themes that emerge. Jack experiences dread, anger, fear of being eaten, and the urge to outwit his foe. In almost all stories about battles with giants there are strong elements of both fear and anger. The fear often involves possibilities of being crushed, dismembered, and devoured. Interestingly, the defeat of the giant is usually engineered by virtue of his clumsiness or stupidity. The small one is portrayed as more agile and clever than the big one. Wolfenstein (1954) has shown in a collection of examples of children's humor that jokes about the size and clumsiness of adults are common. Similar defensive humor can be heard in the comments of adults after encountering someone who is seven or eight feet tall. There is a tendency to want to belittle the big one and make it look as if his size is a handicap rather than an asset.

Anxiety about being incorporated may play a larger element in the fears of the small one than we realize. During psychoanalytic treatment, as individuals try to recall and reconstruct their feelings in early childhood, fantasies about being incorporated are periodically reported. Early fears about the possibility of being eaten up come to light. Images are recalled that concern big things eating little things. Since nature daily presents this "big eat little" paradigm, and since our fairy tales are loaded with plots about witches making a meal of little children, it is not surprising that the small child surrounded by large and powerful figures should, from time to time, have concern about whether he may not find himself consumed. Remember, too, the frequency with which parents playfully tease their children with "I am going to eat you up." In scanning the Rorschach responses of young children I have been impressed with the number of times they refer to animals and other creatures eating each other. Consider further how saturated children's animated cartoons are with incorporative episodes. Every Saturday morning the television screen presents an endless round of encounters in which the victim is swallowed and swallowed again. Even in the safety of church the child is told the tale of the whale swallowing Jonah. Possibly, then, one of the elemental concerns of the small one is that you are vulnerable to being gobbled up by any larger organism that comes along.

The size of your body may be indirectly increased by adding to it the adjoining space; you can spread out by annexing the area around you. People really do think of the space near their bodies as belonging to them and act as if it were a body extension. This has been shown in research dealing with the so-called "body buffer zone." There is a region around each person that he treats as if it were a part of his body substance, and if you intrude into that space he reacts as though you had, without approval, "penetrated" his body. We are all half-aware of this fact and we are careful not to get too close to someone without first receiving a sign of permission to do so. The size of the zone of space that each person reserves in his vicinity depends on a number of things. Most have to do with danger. The greater the potential threat in a situation, the greater the buffer zone the individual appropriates. An analysis of the experiences of men working in remote Arctic stations revealed that as they become increasingly disturbed by the isolation they act more "touchy" about others encroaching on them. For example, a man flares up angrily if someone sits on his bed without permission. He increasingly communicates the message: "This area belongs to me. My person extends to all of my belongings and the space they occupy. Do not enter or you will antagonize me." It is well known that cultures differ in their customs regulating how far you can spread out into the space surrounding your body. Anglo-Saxons extend possession into a relatively wide area and one is supposed to stay quite distant from another during interaction. Others (Italians, for example) treat only a small strip of space as a self-extension and they can stand very close to each other without arousing feelings of intrusion. The space you spread out into will depend upon a number of situational factors. Obviously, you will feel that you own more space around you when sitting alone on a beach than when standing in a crowded subway train. You will probably feel freer to spread out if you are in a position of authority than if you are low in the "peck hierarchy." Being in an aggressive mood will very likely enhance your possessive self-extension, and passivity will have the opposite effect. It is interesting to contemplate, too, what effects modern communications media like television, radio, and telephone may have had on the size of the personal body space. Does the business executive who can in a moment contact any point in the world feel a grandiose sense of spatial extension? I would wonder whether the act of reaching out day after day into the most remote regions of world space does not produce a real and significant impact on one's body concept. (I am not referring to a metaphorical impact, but rather to one that literally changes the experienced dimensions of one's body.) At the very least, I would wonder whether conflicting and puzzling sensations are aroused. The individual knows that his body is located in a particular room, and yet at the same time he is "extending" into spaces thousands of miles away. When you are sitting in a train in a station and the train on the next track begins to move, you may not know for a brief period whether your train or the other one is actually in motion. Because you may be moving but do not have the body experiences that usually accompany movement, it is common to react with sensations of dizziness and strangeness. These sensations can be very vivid, even though you are intellectually aware of the real state of affairs. Analogously, I am suggesting that even though we have a clear intellectual grasp of how long-distance communications media operate, we may still experience (perhaps unconsciously) a sense of strangeness or even depersonalization at the disparity between the static position of our bodies in space and the ease with which we electronically leap through vast distances. The primitive confusions that exist today about such issues are well illustrated by the fears and delusional systems that are common in our schizophrenic casualties. Many psychotics are caught up in puzzled concern about their relationships with electronic communications systems. They wonder whether the image on the TV screen is real; they fear that electronic gadgets are spying on them—literally intruding into their personal space; they experiment with fantasies in which they assign to their own bodies the power to function like electronic instruments (for example, by claiming they can read someone's mind miles away). When technical developments permit people to extend body powers into novel spatial realms, this imposes new burdens on them in their attempts to maintain sensible and viable body concepts. As the individual's body space is technically ballooned he may find himself afflicted with some of the same contradictions that typify institutions in our culture that have become super-big.

If someone is unmistakably shorter than average, almost everyone has the right to feel bigger and to entertain a sense of superiority by laughing "down." The opportunity to be hostile to the short one is maximized when he happens to be a member of some rejected minority group. During World War II the "Little Jap" was a perfect stereotyped target for those who had a special need to bolster their body confidence. I would add that we are pretty well unconscious of how often we "look down" in a depreciating fashion on children because they are small. Obviously, the smallness of children is also cute and endearing, but many adults capitalize on it to reassure themselves of their own psychological stature. Even the kindest of parents is impressed with the power contrast that is obvious in the size difference between his child and himself. A fairly young child who begins to catch up with the physical size of his parents will elicit a different pattern of response from his parents than he did before his stature increased. They will begin to see him as a more equal personage. The adolescent who spurts up to an inch or so taller than his parents finds that he suddenly has a new kind of status with his parents. He may not be much more psychologically mature than he was before his growth spurt, but physical size has a potency all of its own. Indeed, the psychologically immature adolescent who attains mature size often finds himself in a painful dilemma because people expect him to act like an adult before he is inwardly ready to do so.

Anxiety about smallness stems not only from our childhood experiences, in which we discover that the mere fact of being "below" others makes us vulnerable to exploitation, but also to more general *Zeitgeist* factors. Chief among these, I would suggest, is our increasing explicit awareness that the earth is a speck in an infinitely greater universe. As we learn about astral phenomena, it becomes clearly obvious to all people that the world is a tiny detail. Others have pointed out how man's perception of himself as a large central Event has been gradually, and then more dramatically, revised as the Center of Things has shifted from earth, to sun, to Out There. Other reminders of our smallness, such as giant buildings and machines, are only overtones to the larger realization of where we fit into the total picture. The lust for size that is drawing people into producing and building and organizing the biggest This-and-Thats may well represent an epidemic-like response to the shrinkage we have all experienced as information about the real nature of the universe has poured in. Paradoxically, the more that man compensatorily constructs giant objects, the more he fills his environment with reminders of his own smallness.

CHAPTER SEVEN

Creative images from the body

Creative people know that certain situations turn them on and others turn them off. A favorite room or body posture or musical background may help to get the creative process moving. Some artists resort to drugs as a way of producing inspiration, and alcohol has been a popular means for loosening up to get in the mood. As I have reviewed some of the rituals employed by the creative to launch themselves into the stream of improvisation, I have been impressed by the fact that many seem to be based on encouraging certain body sensations and discouraging others. Drugs, alcohol, and favorite postures serve to create a favorite pattern of body perception. Artistic creativity intimately involves the body, not only in the sense that a creative act can only find expression in some muscular, motoric output, but also in terms of the role played by body sensations in motivating and infusing what we call creative fantasies. When a painter who is poised before his canvas begins to mould its surface, there are obviously multiple influences that come together in the final movements of his brush. But there are probably few painters who would deny the considerable shaping effects of the muscular and visceral sensations dominant at that moment. A psychiatrist (Rose, 1963) who has written about this matter points out (p. 786):

> Many painters work with music in the background and describe their motions, posturings, advances to and retreats from the canvas as a kind of ballet. These movements, readily observable in any art class, may reflect or perhaps even facilitate the oscillating projection-introjection which is involved in creating the painting. For example, they may reflect the projection of kinesthetic sensations by which the artist checks the painting as he works and knows whether it "feels right" and how he should make it "work" in order to grow. Many painters describe using their kinesthetic reactions to the figure on the canvas as one body indicator as to whether or not the painting is progressing and balancing well; they literally feel in their muscles, tendons, and joints, in addition to seeing it with an educated eye. When what he sees on the canvas contradicts what his body tells him about the painting, he may even give priority to the judgment of the body, knowing it to be peculiarly direct and intimate.

Rose also relates an anecdote in which Matisse was asked by a friend how he knew which of his many paintings were really good. Matisse replied, "Well, one feels that in the hand."

Leonardo da Vinci was so aware of the importance of one's own body feelings in artistic production that he warned painters not to let their own kinesthetic sensations intrusively falsify their perceptions of figures they were portraying.

There is good evidence that whenever you ask someone to apply his imagination to creating something with meaning from that which has no form of its own, his body feelings find expression. This was originally brought home to me in my work with Cleveland (Fisher and Cleveland, 1968) when we discovered that the images persons conjure up when they are asked to interpret ink blots imaginatively are significantly influenced by their body sensations. If someone is particularly aware of his stomach (for example, when hungry) he will see an unusual number of images of food and other oral things in his ink-blot productions. If someone is unusually aware of the sensations coming from the boundary sheath (skin and muscle) of his body, he will project this pattern of body feeling on to the blots and generate images in which the boundary is dramatized in some way. As noted in the chapter dealing with the body boundary, he will create responses like "cave with rocky walls," "man in armor," and "person covered with a blanket." These responses obviously convey the idea of being covered or protectively contained.

Psychologists have long been interested in what one puts into one's rendering of a human figure. If I draw a human form, how much of myself finds its way into the production? A formal psychological procedure has been developed that is called the Draw-A-Person test. It involves asking the subject or patient to draw a full-length picture of a person. Elaborate procedures have been devised for evaluating the psychological traits that are presumably revealed in the drawing. But what I would particularly like to call to your attention is the fact that such a drawing does mirror body feelings and attitudes. There is formal research evidence that when a person sketches a human form he puts something of his own body feelings and sensations into it. One psychologist (Apfeldorf, 1953) asked persons to draw a human figure and also took full-length photographs of these same people. He demonstrated that judges could match each person's photograph to his figure drawing (which was unidentified) more significantly than by chance. Obviously, each drawing contained some element of the physique or postural style of the person who had sketched it. In a formal way this study verifies what most artists sense: that body feelings and rhythms find representation in their creations.

Rose (1963) describes a woman who had a history of disturbance about the soundness of her body. He reports that her painting style reflected her intense sense of body vulnerability and lack of adequate body boundaries. He indicates (p. 782), "The outstanding feature of her painting . . . is that she would pile up the pigment thickly on the canvas and model it in almost three dimensional forms. Thickening the canvas in this way expressed the . . . need to thicken and thus reinforce her stimulus barrier. . . ." In other words, he interpreted her thick application of paint as a compensatory and symbolic way of expressing her anxiety about the perceived lack of thickness of her own body wall or boundary. I have observed similar phenomena in the works of artists I have known well. I recall one painter who was a defensive, irritable person and very sensitive to possible slight or attack. His muscles were held stiffly and one could see that he maintained them in a chronic state of defense—ready to ward off. When you looked at him you got the impression of someone encased in a tough, muscular capsule. His paintings were obsessively focused on images with body connotations. What was intriguing was that the images almost uniformly portrayed objects that were soft and gelatinous on the inside and crusty, rock-like on the outside. There was a clear analogy between his own "hard" muscle façade and the outer hardness of the images that dominated his canvas.

There is an American artist, Joseph Hirsch, the son of a surgeon, among whose first serious artistic efforts was a lithograph of a man who had lost both of his legs sitting on a little wheeled platform. The figure poignantly conveys the message of a body terribly destroyed and ruined. The artist's concern about body vulnerability comes through loud and clear. However, never again did it appear in his work so openly and explicitly. Instead, he produced a long series of lithographs in which figures were almost invariably portrayed as covered or protected. The people he depicted were variously concealed by a newspaper that was being read or by clothes with an obvious hard, metallic quality or were presented in small spaces with container-like qualities (a phone booth, for example). The body anxiety briefly apparent in one of his first productions gave way to preoccupation with its defensive opposite. I would speculate that his preoccupation with defending the integrity of his own body was repeatedly mirrored in the symbolic forms of body armoring he provided for the figures in his artistic images. Interestingly, in his later work, when he was well beyond middle age, much of the armoring of his figures disappeared and he began to present them nude, without any covering at all. It was as if having successfully survived to a mature age he had sufficiently mastered his anxiety about the body to venture portraying it without a protective façade.

An examination of Picasso's artistic output quickly reveals a deep concern about the integrity of the body. An important and persistent *content* theme of his productions is the violation and mutilation of the body. Mangled animals, protruding entrails, gored horses, and hanged men with terminal erections confront us in his canvases. At a more abstract level, we find that he must, over and over again, take the body apart and put it together in new combinations. A head is simultaneously a front and a side view. Contradictory body aspects are fused. Body areas are grafted into combinations that one might expect to find only in a laboratory devoted to radical genetic experiments. Apropos of his body preoccupation, I was struck by the fact that one of his first major canvases (*Science and Charity*) to win a prize portrayed someone sick in bed and a doctor in attendance. The theme of body incapacity was the central theme. It is therefore interesting to find that Françoise Gilot (1964), Picasso's former mistress, has described him as unusually concerned about certain issues with obvious body implications. Incidentally, she quotes him at one point as saying that the faces of the majority of the human race look like animals. She indicates that he often complained needlessly of being sick and was hypochondriacal about his body. She describes, too, his sensitivity about the dysplastic shape of his body. Although he is of unusually short stature, he has massive shoulders; he dreaded going to a tailor for new clothes because he anticipated that some remark would be made about this incongruity. Therefore, he would wear one or two suits until they were shredding and then buy new clothes only after a good deal of persuasion had been applied. Mlle. Gilot also describes an anxious reluctance on his part to let his hair be cut. One of the more deviant sides of his behavior that she reveals relates to his fear that his children might die. She states that he would awaken her in the middle of the night and insist that she look at the sleeping children to make sure they were still alive. Concern about death is one aspect of concern about corporeal things. To be preoccupied with death themes is, at one level, a reflection of hostility, but in its broadest sense it represents anxiety about whether the body (of self or others) is sufficiently hardy to withstand the bad forces (real or fantasized) impinging upon it.

I would theorize that Picasso's anxiety about whether his children were surviving the night reflects in upsidedown form, and in the spirit of Picasso's own topsy-turvy creations, a theme that we are told was prominent in his own childhood. Sabartes (1948), his biographer, notes that up till adolescence Picasso had enormous difficulty in separating himself from his father. He followed him everywhere and refused to leave him even when it was time to go to school. His father literally had to force him to stay in school, and he would insist on holding on to some possession of his father's while he was in the schoolroom. This behavior might currently be referred to in psychiatric jargon as a school phobia. As was mentioned earlier, there are many children who seem not to be able to distinguish themselves sufficiently from their parents to feel capable of being spatially separated from them—as is required by school attendance. Clinical studies suggest that an important component of this syndrome is the fact that the parents make the child feel that he is a possession, an extension of themselves that cannot survive independently. In other words, there is a profound symbiotic pact. I have proposed that such a symbiosis has strong body components. The parents and child unconsciously perceive their bodies as intermeshed, parts of a system from which parts cannot be individually removed without damaging that system. The child who feels that his body is owned by his parents has a difficult time acquiring a sense of body integrity. He is full of fear that his body cannot function unless it is "connected" to a stronger supporting one. It is just such a fear that one may presume characterized Picasso in his early years. But even after he arrived at old age (when Françoise Gilot described him) he could not conceal his irrational fear that his children would break off their connection to him (by dying). He seems as symbiotically involved with his children as his father probably was with him. Mlle. Gilot notes, in a revealing sidelight on this issue, that Picasso repeatedly insisted on borrowing articles of clothing belonging to his son and holding on to them tenaciously. The "I own part of your body" implications of such behavior are obvious.

Overall, I am hypothesizing that Picasso's body anxieties and his difficulties in learning how to separate his body from that of his father have played a part in the images that are prominent in his creations. He immerses himself in fantasies of body disruption and re-creation[1] as an expression of certain conditions that characterize his body concept. It would be an interesting exercise to explore the possibility that other artistic contemporaries of Picasso who have shown a concern with body distortions in their work had special difficulties as they were growing up in mustering a sense of body integrity and security.

The illustrations that have been presented of body feelings getting into artistic images all involve painters, but they could be compiled from other artistic disciplines.[2] There are contemporary poets, novelists, and playwrights who are obviously very intrigued with the world of body experience. Each, with his own imagery, conveys a particular theme that pulls him. I would call your attention especially to the work of John Updike. His literary output abounds with close scrutiny of the body and body sensations. One of his first major works concerned the world of deteriorating bodies as it exists in a poorhouse. He is especially caught up with boundary phenomena. Concern about the body being penetrated and unprotected appears again and again in his story fantasies. His novel *The Centaur* opens with a vivid image of a teacher who fantasizes he had just had an arrow shot into his foot by a student; it goes on to a sensation-by-sensation account of the pain, the bleeding, and the process of removing the arrow. If one looks at the first page of other novels and stories he has published, the penetration theme is almost immediately in the forefront. In his novel *The Poorhouse* we are, within the first few opening sentences,

---

[1] His fascination with altering the body is also expressed in his playful way of putting on masks and disguising himself.

[2] One can even find examples of creative scientists who describe their ideas and inventions as having body sources. Einstein once said that he could "feel" his mathematical solutions in his musculature.

presented with the following: "An unusual glint of metal *pierced*[3] the lenient wall of Hook's eyes and *struck* into his brain. . . ." One of his short stories ("His Finest Hour") opens as follows: "First they heard, at eight p.m., the sound of a tumbler *shattering*:[3] the crack of the initial concussion, the plump, vegetal pop of the *disintegration*,[3] and the gossip of settling fragments." Still another short story ("Toward Evening") presents this image on the first page: "The cloth beneath his fingers turned moist and kept slipping; Rafe had the hideous notion that *something would break*,[3] and the sack spill, and the woman angrily sink to the pavement as a head in a nest of vacant clothing."

An interesting book has been written by a psychoanalyst (Greenacre, 1955) concerning the role of the body image in the works of Lewis Carroll and Jonathan Swift. She was impressed with the fact that both of these writers were, in their most famous works, greatly taken up with the matter of body deviance and transformation. In Carroll's *Alice's Adventures in Wonderland* he takes Alice through one episode after another in which her body is radically changed in size, and she meets characters who have wonderfully grotesque bodies. Greenacre observes (p. 217):

> *Alice's Adventures in Wonderland* is replete with descriptions of bizarre and unassimilated body feelings. . . . Alice's body becomes enormous and suddenly elongated or collapses and shrinks sadly. Her neck particularly becomes so serpent-like that she is actually mistaken for a serpent hiding in a tree. Her arm and leg, each in turn, seem strange, far away, and hardly part of herself in their grotesquely enlarged form.

Similarly, Swift's Gulliver encounters in his travels the Lilliputians, the towering giants of Brobdingnag, and the Yahoos, who are unspeakably filthy in their body habits. He is caught up in worlds of outrageous body events. Greenacre concluded, after a detailed analysis of the lives of Carroll and Swift, that their preoccupation with body distortion reflected their early difficulties in making sense of their own bodies. Both were unable to accept the masculine phallic aspects of their bodies. Both were disgusted by their body openings and particularly disturbed by anal functions. They seemed to view the body as alien and were chronically ill at ease with the biological stuff of which they were composed. In their story fantasies they were able to pour out the flood of disturbing body sensations with which they lived.

[3] Italics inserted for emphasis.

They were indirectly able to experiment with different visions of the body and even to charm others into approving the most extreme of these visions.

Many other writers could be cited who display unusual preoccupation with themes of body transformation and mutilation in their story plots and who, in their personal lives, were obviously caught up with a succession of disturbing body events. Two that are widely known are Edgar Allen Poe and Robert Louis Stevenson. Poe's stories abound, of course, in endless fascination with death and mutilation. They sometimes are built around events involving the strange behavior of a single part of the body (as in "The Tell-Tale Heart"). Parallel to this, one finds that Poe's life was filled with an unbelievable number of tragic encounters with illness and death in those who were close to him. Similarly, Stevenson wrote the story of "The Strange Case of Dr. Jekyll and Mr. Hyde," which has as one of its central themes the possibility of a man's body being radically transformed into a bad, ugly object. Interestingly, Stevenson himself indicated that the story evolved from a disturbing dream he had one night after he had had a severe lung hemorrhage. He suffered from tuberculosis from childhood and had chronically experienced his body as a painful, disagreeable thing. It is not surprising, then, that he should have been concerned with themes of body instability and ugliness.

If an imaginative production catches some of the body feelings and distortions of its creator, it may set up sympathetic vibrations in others. The person viewing a painting or reading a novel may find that the body experiences condensed within it "fit with" his own. His like or dislike of the artistic production may hinge upon whether the "fit" has positive or negative implications. The body distortions embodied in one artist's work may sharply and unpleasantly remind certain viewers of similar distortions in their own body concepts. The body references contained in another work may be comforting to other viewers because they give good messages about being able to master body anxiety. The person who is alarmed about the fragility of his body boundary may find it supportive to absorb himself in a painting in which the artist has portrayed the human figures as soundly protected (for example, clad in shiny armor). Greenacre (1955), after analyzing the body distortions in the work of Lewis Carroll, suggested that one reason why the tale of Alice had so universally been admired was that it turned the spotlight on wishes and anxieties involving the body that all persons struggle with, but that it did so in the protective safety of a torrent of humor and images so ridiculous that they are funny rather than dangerous. Real body threats are portrayed in a setting so unreal that they lose their disturbing charge. They are publicly declared to exist but simultaneously put off at a laughable distance.

Artistic productions obviously differ in how much they evoke perceptible body sensations. A short story may call up vague mood sensations; the stance of a figure in a painting may set up sympathetic feelings in our own musculature; and the sound of a rousing musical march may evoke massive rhythmic muscle feelings. I would, in fact, speculate that music exceeds all other creative productions in its power to influence body experience. Music not only mobilizes profound patterns of body sensations but does so with unique quickness. Listening to just a few bars of music may transform the feel of your body. If so, it would be logical to consider the possibility that when the composer is creating music his body feelings play a larger role in what he is doing than such feelings usually do in other creative endeavors. I would speculate that the successful composer has learned to code and translate his body sensations into sound patterns. The rhythms of music may be metaphors for body-sensation rhythms involving either parts or the total of the body. This view is not meant to downgrade the importance of cognitive and technical skills in composing but only to highlight the possible special prominence of body imagery in generating melodies. It is intriguing to speculate that composers may be "tuned in" on different sectors of their own bodies and that the idiosyncratic sound each creates reflects his specialization. One composer might be attracted to the variations in his muscle sensations and therefore give us music with a "muscular" sound. Another might be caught up with the incessant throb of his heart deep in his body, becoming more and less loud as other surface body sensations wax and wane, and unconsciously mirror this in music constructed around the shifting, swelling, and retreat of a complex matrix of sounds. Note, too, that much of today's popular music is devoted to what it feels like to experience the ecstasy and the loss of love. It is my impression that intuitively there is great popular awareness of the power of music to influence body experience. It is common for people to relieve muscle tension or some particular brand of unpleasant inner sensations by listening to a musical favorite. They have learned by trial and error that certain kinds of music do good things to their body feelings. In fact, some seem to get addicted to musical input as a way of bolstering their body perceptions. Witness the growing custom of transporting a portable radio wherever one goes (even in the street) and loudly immersing oneself in an unending sequence of musical selections, which are rather similar in flavor. In all cultures some version of music is used to blanket the environment—to soothe or excite the body. An individual can also supply himself with portable music by whistling, humming, and singing. There are people who hum melodies to themselves whenever they are alone. They seem to get considerable reassurance from the repetition of a few favorite themes. Of course, in this instance there may be additional reassurance in the feedback from activating the mouth area and hearing the sound of one's own voice. Just as a full stomach may feel good, the rhythmic movement of mouth and tongue may have "All is well" or "I am all right" connotations.

The very question of whether a person is willing to open himself to any species of artistic communication may depend on body attitudes. There are people who avoid and screen out the aesthetic. They do not want to expose themselves to information that might have hidden messages. Once you decide to look at a painting or to read a novel you have opened yourself to the potential inputs they contain. We have found hints in some of our research (Fisher and Greenberg, 1972) that fundamental attitudes about body penetration may play a role in how people respond to music. In one study we discovered that the greater the masculinity of a woman's orientation (as measured by a personality questionnaire) the more likely she is to respond to both exciting and calm music with feelings of anxiety. The feminine woman was able to sit and listen to music for an extended period without feeling anxious, but this was not true of her more masculine counterpart. We speculated that this difference had something to do with the contrasting attitudes of men and women to being penetrated. The feminine mode is to be open and even to welcome penetration of her body in sexual terms. The masculine mode is to be guarded and to prevent rigorously the intrusion into one's body of anything foreign. When you commit yourself to listen for a period of time to a musical selection you are, in a sense, passively allowing the music to gain entry to you. It is our view that the more masculine the psychological stance of the women we studied the more likely they were to perceive the music that was "gaining entry" to them as an intrusion and therefore to feel anxious about the implications.

In this vein, it is relevant to call your attention to another study in which we were trying to find out what types of parents are most likely to bring up a child who has a clear, secure image of his body boundaries and who is not chronically concerned about the dangers of being penetrated. We found only a few parental attributes whose presence would predict the quality of the child's boundary, but of these few, one that emerged was the degree to which the parents demonstrate an aesthetic attitude toward the world. If the mother and father placed value on the enjoyment of the aesthetic (music or painting, for example), their children were typified by secure boundaries. My interpretation of this finding is that parents who seek out aesthetic experiences are people who are not afraid to open themselves to ambiguous stimuli and who in fact welcome such exposure. Through this attitude they may communicate to their children a sense of security about potential penetration. Perhaps they minimize the danger, and focus on the pleasure, of allowing interesting and novel things to gain entry to self.

Several theorists have said that the creative artist has to be uniquely able to open himself with trust to the stimuli that impinge upon him from "out there." Presumably, if he is to arrive at truly original perceptions, he has to absorb freely and accumulate experiences that can then be integrated in novel ways. However, anecdotal reports suggest that some creative people find the process of opening themselves to be seriously threatening; they become anxious and caught up with sensations of vulnerability and of losing control. In fact, some artists apparently find the opening-up experience to be one that puts them on the edge of psychosis. In the letting-down of their boundaries they lose self-delineation and have unrealistic sensations of merging with other objects in their vicinity. Of course, the truth is that we know little about what happens to the psychological economy of the artist when he is in the throes of creating new images. It would be interesting, although a bit sacrilegious, to measure the state of the body boundary and various tension systems in a series of artists as they become progressively more caught up in new productions. I believe that given the proper preparation this could be done without killing the creative sequence itself.

Returning again to the role of body experience in creativity, it is interesting that several writers who have studied the careers of famous creative people have been impressed with their early unusual investment in body sensations. Greenacre has been most vocal about this point. She says that even as children the creative are quick to get into states of body excitement and to be carried along by rhythmic body sensations. She suggests that they are unusually sensitive to their body states and become motivated to integrate these states with the non-body stimuli (from "out there") that impinge upon them. Roe (1953), who studied the careers of famous scientists, made an intriguing observation about creative theoretical physicists. She noted that an unusual number of them had suffered from severe childhood illnesses that had made them invalids for quite a time. She wondered if this kind of body experience might not disillusion them about the body and cause them to reject it as a standard for evaluating experiences. Further, she speculated that this might account for the theoretical physicist's superior ability to manipulate size concepts. That is, if he could abstract his size concepts from their relationship to his own body he would be freer to manipulate them in theoretical ways. I think Roe's observation about the early illness pattern of the physicists is an important one, but I do not agree with her interpretation of it. It seems to me that if you are sick for a long time your body becomes the most important object in your world and you are likely to attach exaggerated significance to body sensations. Your body discomfort pervades your thinking and judgment. Perhaps the theoretical physicists show superiority in manipulating spatial concepts because they were so intensively plunged into the experience of their own bodies, which are after all our first and most basic compass points for spatial directionality. There is, in fact, one recent study that indicated that children who were made more familiar with the spatial dimensions of their bodies improved in their ability to make spatial discriminations in other non-body situations. In any case, what I particularly want to stress about Roe's observations is the fact that the creative physicists had a history of early severe illness, which might have turned them intensely toward body experience.

Roe (1951) also studied a group of the most eminent creative men in biology. She found that a large percent of them had suffered the loss of their mothers in childhood (usually through death), and in general their early family relationships seemed somewhat confused and insecure. She found, too, that as adults they were rather detached from people and deeply invested in their mission to innovate. They were, without respite, devoted to the search for new ideas. The fact that so many had experienced the death of their mothers in their early years would indirectly fit the idea that the creative grow up under circumstances that would make them hyperaware of the body. Surely their early contact with death in their own mothers would highlight the centrality of the body in human affairs.

Roe and others have observed that the creative tend to assign much more importance to their innovating than they do to their relationships with other people. They have a singleminded devotion to bringing forth their new visions. I wonder whether this has something to do with a conviction on their part that they cannot count on others to play a nurturant role to them—that they must nurse and coax out of themselves whatever potential they possess. Also, if they early had experiences (with death, illness, and intrusively symbiotic parents, for example) that tell them that the very process of being or existing as an independent entity is difficult, they may defensively feel the need to cultivate that which represents growth in self. By nurturing what is new or creative within themselves they can deny the possibility of decline and death. In their devotion to cultivating their own creativity they are like gardeners who carefully tend a delicate plant that looks as if it might have trouble surviving. Their own fantasies are treated like little babies that need to be cuddled and fed. It is well known, too, that the artist and the inventor often view their creations as objects that will survive them and give them a future immortality. In this way they can get beyond the limitations of the vulnerable body. Each new idea represents "new growth," continuation as opposed to decline. A number of psychoanalysts have described a tendency for creative persons to become depressed for a while after completing a major work and then to regain their spirits after starting a new creative enterprise. In other words, they feel down and in a state of decline unless they are actively cultivating new ideas. One psychiatrist even reported that becoming pregnant (which is about as literally creative as one can be) seemed to be a way of escaping severe depression for some women.

I have conducted several studies that turned up the fact that persons with strong artistic or literary interests are particularly likely to have high generalized body awareness. These studies involved college students. Their interests were measured with formal questionnaires and also by asking them to list ten occupations which "you consider most attractive or interesting." Their overall amount of body awareness (Body Prominence) was determined by a technique based on the number of times an individual refers to the body when he is asked to list on a sheet of paper "20 things that you are aware of or conscious of right now." Details of this technique are available elsewhere (Fisher, 1970). Consistent positive correlations were found between degree of body awareness and amount of interest in artistic and aesthetic matters. This is one of the first bits of scientific evidence that an artistic orientation is tied to a special awareness of one's own body. It is, of course, congruent with the speculations of those who see body experience as an important source of that which goes into artistic expression.

It will take a good deal more evidence before we can say with any assurance that the artistically oriented, creative individual is more tuned in on his body than the average person, but let us for the moment assume that the scattered bits of evidence are encouraging. If so, what kind of model of this relationship can we construct? Why should heightened awareness of one's body play a part in becoming artistically creative? I would propose that basic to an explanation is the fact that in most cultures the body represents elements in the world that are poorly controlled, unpredictable, and sloppy or dirty. It is the body that is identified with the flash of an overpowering emotion, the flow of blood and urine, and the possibility of extraordinarily deviant or embarrassing behavior. The child learns that many of his troubles stem from the fact that his body won't do what his parents expect of it. He is not encouraged to have fun with his body or to become absorbed in it. This is especially true if he is a male. Rather, the emphasis is placed on gaining control over and automatizing the body —getting it sufficiently disciplined so that the child can turn to the big task of learning to fill his social roles. In other words, the body represents the rawness of nature, the non-respectable, and the potentially uncontrollable. It stands in opposition to the Establishment. So, if circumstances cause a child to turn to his own body with special intensity and to enjoy or be fascinated with what he experiences, this may be a first major step in deviating from the accepted way of looking at things. By becoming unusually sensative to his own body he breaks with the traditional assumptions about where it is proper to focus his attention. At that point he has shifted to a relatively less normative and more novel viewpoint. Further, once he becomes "body sensitive" his experiences are less controllable by the people who are trying to socialize him. The conforming child who turns away from his body will find all kinds of signposts (parental injunctions, school routine) to tell him from hour to hour where he should be looking and what he should be thinking about. His attention will be controlled and normalized by the various classes of uniform stimuli that will be kept before him. But the experiences of the child who has learned to tune in on his body cannot be so easily homogenized. The sensations coming from his body are his own, they shift and fluctuate, and they have their own unique patterns. Even when he is in places where others are telling him pretty much what he should be experiencing (in school, for example), his body feelings buffer what is coming from "out there" and add a unique individual coloring to it all. The child who has discovered and seeks the rich experiences of his own body is already embarked on a more individualistic trajectory. He is already adopting a style of perception that favors seeing things differently—and more originally.

There are a number of factors that might turn a child toward special interest in his own body. One of the most obvious is serious or extended illness. The sick child is probably made acutely aware of his body, and he finds that his parents are similarly aware of it. Suddenly, his body becomes the center of events and may, if the sickness is of sufficient duration or intensity, cause a major shift in his division of attention between corporeal events and those "out there." This may occur despite the unpleasantness of being sick. The suffering in a story or the ugly image in a painting, although disturbing, can be fascinating. Also, one must keep in mind that when the child is sick he gets tremendous gratification out of being the center of attention and escaping his routine responsibilities. Indeed, it is even possible to conceive how, in this respect, the sick child might begin to equate the world of body experience with an escape from all that is routine and expected by the authorities.

There are other ways in which the body could acquire dramatic interest to the child. He might have an unusual parent who would enthusiastically direct his attention to his body and perhaps by example indicate the potential rewards of involvement with your own body universe. Or he might have a parent who so savagely denies him the right to look at, or think about, his body that he defiantly turns to his own sensations. He might do this not only to express his anger at being overcontrolled but also because he senses in his parent's overdetermined behavior that what is being forbidden to him has great illicit appeal. There is promise that the forbidden area of experience may be very rewarding in its juicy badness. One could enumerate further possibilities. For example, the child living in a lonely, isolated way might find that his own body is practically the only available object to which he can relate meaningfully. Or there might be someone in the child's immediate family who chronically suffered with a body defect and who, in his preoccupation with his disablement, would give the message that the bodily sphere is paramount.

As has been stated, once the child is launched into close encounters with his own body experiences, he is straying from the conventional path. He is seeing the world "differently." This would in itself provide some of the novelty of perspective that is a constituent of being original and creative. But what else comes out of this turning to one's body that would contribute to an artistic orientation? The second factor I would underscore is that it gives the individual an investment in what he generates from within. In attending to the sensations coming from his body he not only develops skill in detecting new patterns in himself but attaches importance to these internal phenomena. He sharpens his skills in making sense of his inward feelings and also views the process of knowing about his internal states as a serious enterprise. It is doubtful that anyone can be creative unless he prizes and honors the cues, sensations, and half-formed feelings that are precursors to new ideas. He has to value the inward-turning and inward-searching game.

It is probably also true that being close to your own body experiences makes it more possible to learn the extent to which your interpretations of events are shaped by how you "feel." You get repeated intimations of how your view of things depends upon the framework of your internal emotions. The fact that your inner feelings affect your interpretations becomes obvious. The portrayal of such relativity is a central aim of the artist. He is usually intent on conveying the interaction between an emotional perspective and an object or event outside of himself.

Finally, I would stress the fact that there are few, if any, ways of making direct contact with the real stuff of nature that compare with observation of your own body. So many of the natural, biological processes are screened from view. Only rarely is one able to become intensively acquainted with the uncovered, unconcealed body of another. Body products of others are carefully hidden. Death is relegated to little rooms in a hospital. Even eating is shrouded in etiquette. Only by watching his own body does the average individual get a direct, naïve, and intensive experience with the nude frame and its fluids, products, rhythms, and smells. You get to know about some of the basics of nature primarily through what you witness happening to your body. I think this bears on artistic creativity because such creativity is so often directed at facing up to nature without pretence. To be able to look boldly and without restraint at natural events as they occur is increasingly a concern of the artist—and obviously of the creative in many other disciplines.

If the ideas just outlined are valid, then the turning away from your own body, which is so common, suppresses a big reservoir of potential creativity. A lot of people who could get a creative charge out of their own body experiences are not doing so. I wonder if this does not contribute to the widespread sense of body dissatisfaction. So many people feel that their bodies lack something. They spend a good deal of time trying to improve their bodies and are rarely happy with the results. There are not many other sectors of human activity in which dissatisfaction is so rampant and persistent. Perhaps this is one reflection of the individual's feeling that the potentialities of his body experiences are grossly unrealized.

Why have so few women achieved recognition as artistic innovators? I have shown that women are more body aware than men, more comfortable in dealing with body sensations, and generally less anxious about potential body damage. Why does this greater ease with body experiences not result in a greater ability to channel them into creative imagery? Of course, it could be argued that women have been unable to realize their creative potential simply because they are confined to subordinate feminine roles. One could say they have not been as free as men to explore and try their hand at novel things. This line of explanation may contain a lot of truth. But at the same time, I would like to point out that many creative male artists have been able to do their work only under the most radically restricting circumstances. They have often had to produce their new images in the face of formidable circumstances (for example, getting no economic reward or being labeled as a bad deviant). Is it possible that the decisive factor in fostering greater image-creativity in men than women is the fact that men are more restricted than women in how they can "listen to" and express their body experiences? Girls are given a fair amount of permission to be open to emotional feelings, to attend to their bodies, and to experiment with body appearance (by means of new clothes fashions and cosmetics, for example). But boys can show interest in their bodies only through the channel of strenuous muscular exertion, such as in work or athletic games. They are regarded as feminine even if they show too much investment in vigorous body movements like expressive dancing! The boy finds the world of body experience considerably more closed to him than does the girl. In other words, girls have a greater number of conventional ways of expressing their body perceptions. To be close to the body psychologically is a more normal state of affairs for them. A man who takes the path of living close to his body experiences does by that very act declare himself to be a deviant. He has to be somewhat of a cultural mutant to begin with. Further, since he cannot express his body interests in conventional ways, he has greater incentive to do so in novel forms. These factors may combine to increase the likelihood of an end product that is novel and original (creative). A woman who can create a new human inside herself and who can, during the process, spend months attending to the drama of her changing body sensations may simply not need other modes for realizing the world of her body.

If the artistic creation has a sizeable body-image component, what impact does it have on its creator? When an artist looks at the figures on his canvas does he react to the body-image information it conveys about him? Perhaps the repeated mirroring back of self-images contained in the artistic product is a part of the motivation for creative activity. The artist painting a self-portrait is obviously concerned with how he looks and gets a chance, through the portrait, to study a particular version of his appearance that intrigues him. But even the artist who has put his body image into a painting in a more concealed fashion may unknowingly get important feedback related to body feelings from looking at his creation. It will be recalled that there is scientific evidence that people can respond to representations of their bodies even when they are not consciously aware that they are doing so. A person may see a picture of his hands and not know that they are his, but when he is asked to describe the hands he says more favorable things about them than he does about the pictured hands of others. Similarly, an artist may, without conscious awareness, see parts of himself in one of his compositions and be affected by the experience.[4] Perhaps most creative products contain such representations of one's body feelings. Whether it be a piece of music, a poem, a novel mathematical equation, or a new machine, the product could conceivably carry the imprint of the body perspective of the creator. It may seem farfetched to suggest that a product like a new machine can reflect the inventor's body feelings, but note that Tausk (1933), a psychiatrist, was impressed by the fact that when schizophrenic patients delusionally invent machines that they imagine are producing forces that act on their bodies from a distance, they assign unique properties to them that turn out upon careful analysis to resemble aspects of their own bodies. Conceivably, the machine devised by an inventor may, in its shape or function, duplicate an important sphere of body experience for him. Obviously, the shape of a machine is determined to an important extent by engineering necessities, but I would presume there are sufficient mechanical alternatives so that preferences could be affected by more subjective elements in the inventor's outlook. If the created ob-

---

[4] Several psychologists have presented clinical evidence that even when an individual draws a picture of an object like a tree or house he puts representations of himself into it.

ject mirrors back to the artist or innovator certain attitudes he enter-
tains toward his body, what light might this throw on the creative process itself?

Aside from the obvious gains of creativity that have to do with
winning fame and fortune, there may be some that involve mastering
and reveling in body experiences. We can only guess about this matter.
But consider a few possibilities:

1. Perhaps the person who is caught up and excited with his
inner world of body experiences does not feel authenticated until he
gets a chance to give some form to them in a product that others can
see and admire. He cannot get direct recognition for the special excitement of his own inner sensations. No one else can feel these sensations. He needs to convert them into an external, concrete object before he can persuade others that something special is going on inside
him. One psychoanalyst, Greenacre (1958), has astutely noted that
many creative people feel like imposters until they get widespread
recognition. They do not expect others to understand or believe the
richness of what is occurring within them, and so their life task becomes that of making it all visible and publicly acknowledged.

2. The creative product that mirrors back self-representations
may be a way to get self-affirmation. It may have the same functional
meaning as repeatedly watching yourself in the mirror to be sure that
you look all right. An artist may see in each of his canvases images that
tell him: "Yes, you do exist. Your body is significant and alive and a
solid thing." This sort of reassurance might be important if an individual has grown up in an environment in which there was great
body insecurity.

3. In his output the creative person may seek to heal his anxiety
about a specific part of his body. There are painters and sculptors who
seem preoccupied with certain body areas more than with others. They
may focus on the head or the eyes or the breasts. Also, they may, by
omission of given body parts, convey their need to blot out awareness
of such parts. In his repeated encounter with a specific body part in
his work the artist has a chance to ponder it and to desensitize himself
to its threatening implications.

It is well known that man is inclined to interpret the world physi-
ognomically. The term physiognomic refers to a way of looking out at
things and assigning qualities to them that duplicate our own body
feelings. The poet may describe a wave as "excited" or "angry." He may
perceive a rock formation as "tired" or a cloud as "agitated." The myths

of most cultures conceptualize the phenomena of nature as imbued with human qualities. Storms, sunsets, and the growth of crops are attributed to agents who have human-like form. Man has for a long time not been able to restrain his inclination to endow everything with his own body vitality. However, with increasing scientific knowledge it has become more difficult to do this sort of thing without being blatantly irrational. One can no longer sanely attribute a sunrise to a god figure in human form who drives a marvelous chariot. It is true that one can still believe in the existence of A God, but his sphere of influence has been increasingly narrowed (to the Day of Creation) and less and less linked with the occurrence of specific, current, natural phenomena. The rational man's universe has been put in the frame of gravitation, atomic structure, and the interaction of impersonal vectors. At the same time man has been under pressure from his own moralistic rules and the nature of twentieth-century mechanization to regulate his own body and to reduce it to a not very important cog in a larger system. In other words, man's body has shifted from being the center of the universe to a quite subsidiary role.

I am reviewing this course of events because I think it bears on the revolution of art in this century. As one surveys the work of Ensor, Munch, Vincent van Gogh, the Expressionists, and the Surrealists, one can see an increasing animistic orientation—which is quite analogous to that found earlier in most cultures. There has been more and more of Mickey-Mouse-like animation. The still life has become increasingly full of tensions that are like an excited body. In Vincent van Gogh's painting, inanimate forms like the sun or a hill or the space in a room press upon us like feeling, quasi-protoplasmic things. Abstract forms on Kandinsky's canvases have a life of their own. They are as alive as the talking tree in an animated cartoon. The objects in Dali's world have the postures and states of human moods. Inanimate things on his canvas can be dying. Even Pollack's color conglomerations advertise the emotion and vitality that we associate with the feel of the aroused human body. I would argue that this wave of animism represents a revolt against the downgrading of the human body. It is a way of declaring, "My body feelings are important. They not only occur within my body space, but affect everything in my world. My body is the center of events and not unimportantly on the periphery. The way in which my body feels colors everything I see." This is a world view that states that man's own sensations are paramount. It is a view that does not confine body feelings to a small receptacle but that regards them as being as pervasive as gravitational waves. Even when Picasso dismembers the body, he makes it the dominant theme in the picture. He saturates the entire vista with body properties.

It has been said that artists foretell in their paintings and other art forms changes that will sweep over a culture. They have been described as the sensitive antennae of the total social organism that detect what is up ahead. If there is any truth to this idea, I would see it as deriving in part from the body sensitivity that resides in the artistic. We are trained from childhood to view the things happening to us through selective lenses. We learn to accept certain ways of living even if they are unpleasant and unsatisfying. We invent all kinds of verbal rules and rationalizations to help us give meaning to the style of living we have accepted. But no matter what elaborate, intellectualized perspectives we invent to explain our own behavior, the body continues in an elemental way to register its response to what life is bringing. If life conditions are disturbing or threatening, they will register in sensations of body discomfort—even if there are simultaneous verbal announcements about how "nice" things are. Most people have learned to avoid confrontation with their bad body feelings. They either ignore them or attribute them to some version of illness. But those who are sensitive to their body experiences and who have skill in interpreting them will understand the significance of their bodily discomfort, and this understanding will find outlet in their creative images. These images will tell the story that certain untenable conditions of living exist or that certain assumptions about the current human state are wrong. In this telling they foretell significant change because when conditions are such that they are producing widespread discomfort (even if not consciously acknowledged by most people) they are generating tensions that will begin to undermine the existing cultural structures.

CHAPTER
EIGHT

Motionless body

It may not be a coincidence that the two things we keep most secret from our children are birth and death. Somehow, we do not want them to be directly confronted with how they were created or how they will be extinguished. Perhaps the beginning and the end are linked in their common reference to the fact that there are boundaries to the state of being alive. There is a time of body existence and a time of body non-existence. To master the fear generated by this bare statement has strained the ingenuity of every known society. To witness death is to know that your own body is vulnerable to death. If someone else's body can become nothing, so can your own. An amazing repertory of strategies has been developed across the world to buffer this recognition. Elaborate myths have been invented that portray death as only temporary and leading to rebirth in a new and marvelous place. Most of the concepts of immortality, whether they involve the Resurrection or Valhalla, make use of such myths. Religious forces have taken the lead in trying to make death palatable. They have assured the average man that his death is part of a meaningful scheme of things, that his soul will live on, that he will get his rewards beyond the grave, that death

147

only betokens joining with God, that reincarnation is inevitable, and so forth. There are some cultures that have chosen to defend themselves against the threat of death by hiding it. Our own Western society provides the best example. There are so many obvious ways in which we screen the rawness of death from sight. We rarely talk about death. The deceased is immediately whisked off to the funeral parlor, and his preparation for burial is left to the expert professional undertaker, who dresses him up and creates the illusion he is in a state of slumber rather than dead. The illusion that death does not exist is enhanced by the declining death rate and the consequent decrease in the frequency with which unpredictable casualties occur in any individual family. Another way of hiding death is to segregate the elderly into institutions and hospitals where their dying will be out of sight. Those most potentially ripe for dying are assigned cubicles in places where only specialized nursing personnel are likely to have much contact with them, and there are smooth, well-worked-out procedures for disposing of their remains as unobtrusively as possible. The banishment of death is also reinforced by the siren-like promises of science that it will soon be able to master the major diseases and ailments. There is a half-belief, widely accepted, that soon all serious defects of the body will be repairable. If so, death can be put off—for a long, long time. There is the implication that death will no longer be obligatory. It will be quasi-accidental. Or it will be due to carelessness and neglect. Presumably, people do not have to die if they avoid cholesterol, refrain from smoking, see their physicians regularly, fill up on the right vitamins, and so forth. When all else fails, you can always get a heart transplant or a renal dialysis. If death can be conceptualized as avoidable and subject to the control of omnipotent science, it becomes psychologically more distant. It is less a fact of personal inevitability and more the concern of a vast intellectual apparatus. Of course, in that sense the defense pattern is not so different from religious strategies that instruct the individual that his death is programmed by God and when it occurs will be a meaningful part of a vast game plan.

It should be noted that while there is less *direct* contact with death in our society than there used to be, indirect confrontation has been many times multiplied. An evening of television viewing brings more messages about death in a few hours than most people previously had to absorb in a month. After the news broadcast that gives the box score, for the entire world, of the more spectacular deaths of the day (due to floods, crashes, wars, concentration camps, and self-immolation), there usually follow a succession of dramatic programs that average several deaths each. The evening closes with another news summary of the latest mayhem. This process is duplicated in various ways in radio broadcasts, newspapers, and popular magazines. Each of us is bombarded almost hour by hour by images of death. Sometimes, as on television, the images are vivid, bloody pictures. But these encounters differ from those of a past time because they are largely impersonal. They involve people we have never met. They are quantitatively great but personally distant. Perhaps we learn to defend against them so well that they have little influence on our fantasies and behavior. But I doubt this. I read an anecdote in which a teacher talked about the reactions of a group of young children to the news that John Kennedy had been assassinated. She poignantly described one child who lay down on the floor, closed his eyes, and pretended to be dead (refusing to speak) for a long period of time. This child was obviously captured and moved by the image of death he had received in the day's news. It is likely that many others are equally moved, although they do not show their feelings so openly and dramatically. But even as I make this point, I would not argue that the impersonal death messages from television compare in intensity with those you get from actually being in the presence of the corpse. This is often brought home to the medical student when he begins to become acquainted with the cadaver assigned to him. He discovers that this brand of closeness to death is powerful stuff. He not infrequently goes through a period of being upset, has bad dreams, and experiences strange and puzzling sensations. If you will introspect about your own feelings the last time you attended a funeral you will be able to empathize with the adaptation required of the medical student.

The image of death is an attack on all of the defenses that the individual laboriously constructs to bolster his body security. It challenges the soundness of his boundaries and implies that he cannot prevent destructive intrusion. In a more tense way, it duplicates the effect of the sight of a crippled or "different" kind of body (black, for example). To participate in funeral rites is to realize that your body is subject to the same unthinkable transformations encountered in monster movies. Of course, even more starkly, it suggests that your body can simply disintegrate and vanish. Many burial practices are designed to counter the disappearance of the body. Embalming is a good example. The use of massive, fortified caskets designed to keep out the worms is another. The pyramids are a supreme example. Even cultures that fervently believe in an immortal soul have tried hard to create the illusion that when the body is put into the ground it will endure in its basic physical form.

Fear of the corpse is found everywhere. Folklore is filled with tales about the dead who return to do horrible things to the living. The vampire myths capture the inner terror that plagues people about the destructive potential of the corpse. Built into many funeral rites are ceremonies designed to keep the dead from coming back. The Hopi draw lines across the path leading from the place of burial to the village. These lines magically block the dead one from using the path. He cannot return. Why is there so much fear that the corpse will do bad things? There may be a number of reasons, but one I would especially single out has to do with the simple fact that the corpse becomes a mirror image of what could happen to anyone. In other words, our fears that the dead one will return to do us harm may reflect our feeling that death could return again and that we could be the victims. The corpse symbolizes the inevitable resurgence of a force that can destroy us. Of course, there may also be other reasons for fearing the dead one. You may unconsciously feel that you were unfair to him while he was alive and that he has good reason to seek revenge. You may be angry at him for dying and deserting you, and the very intensity of your anger may suggest that he in turn feels the same way about you.

We know that our culture is anxiously preoccupied with the threat of death, but how much time do we individually spend worrying about it? Is there a lot of conscious preoccupation with it? Is the concern largely unconscious? Several investigators have tried to deal with these questions. They have interviewed people about their attitudes toward death, administered questionnaires, and also used techniques for exploring unconscious fantasies about dying. Generally, it has turned out that most people deny much conscious concern about death. They indicate that they do not often think about such matters. Interestingly, the older an individual is or the greater his religiousness the less likely he is to state that the thought of death alarms him. Older people, especially, seem to be more gracefully resigned to the death process than are the younger. But despite the general tendency for people to deny anxiety about death, indirect approaches have come up with quite another picture. If you ask people to respond to words with direct death significance (grave, for example) or even those with tangential death meaning (depart, last journey), they show clear signs of anxiety (as indicated by physiological measures). If you study the spontaneous stories that people create, you find appreciable involvement with themes of dying. One investigator (Anthony, 1940) observed a remarkable amount of anxiety about death in a sample of children. When she asked them to complete a series of brief story themes, she found that 50 percent of them introduced references to death, despite the fact that the original themes contained no such references. Several attempts have been made to determine if certain kinds of people are more afraid of death than other kinds. Studies of this topic are still in an elementary stage. But there are suggestions that persons who are inclined to be depressed or preoccupied with hypochondriacal body complaints are particularly anxious about death (Fulton, 1965). Interestingly, it has also been found that those with strong dependency needs (who feel they need close parasitic-like ties to survive) are high in death anxiety. Some evidence exists, although far from conclusive, that the greater a person's overall sense of body insecurity (especially his concern with suffering body damage) the more likely he is to be threatened by the thought of dying. This indirectly fits a favorite speculation among psychoanalysts that unusual concern with death is a reflection of castration anxiety. The term *castration anxiety* refers to the fear that important figures in one's life (the father, for example) will inflict damage, particularly upon the genitals, as punishment for wrongdoing or opposing them.

How do children become aware of death? How do they incorporate it into their concept of their own bodies and of the world in general? Empirical studies demonstrate (Anthony, 1940; Piaget, 1929) that up to the age of five the average child has only hazy notions about it. He has difficulty at first in even distinguishing the animate from the inanimate. Anything that moves seems alive to him. He has trouble in deciding whether or not a candle flame is alive because of its dancing movements. When something is motionless it can be classified as not living or dead. Gradually, the child witnesses phenomena that educate him about life versus death, but it is difficult for him to comprehend the idea that death is a natural or final thing. He thinks of death as primarily due to accident or disease or violence. It is not inevitable and it is reversible. He assumes that things that die can, by suitable manipulation, be brought back to life. To die is somewhat like going to sleep. You can be re-awakened. This, of course, is the basic concept that most cultures have tried to maintain in their myths and religious systems. The idea that the dead can be revived in some form is a return to the child's original view of it all. Up to the age of nine interpretations of death remain magical and unreal. Dying is attributed to arbitrary actions by evil things or people. According to some, it is also especially likely to be tied in with matters of anger and fantasies of desertion. That is, people die because they want to go away or get rid of you. It is only around the age of nine that the child seems to crystallize the adult concept that death is part of a natural impersonal cycle. Incidentally, the child's earlier assumption that dying is caused by an evil agent that has for special reasons singled out the person in question is sometimes adopted by an entire culture. There are societies that have been studied (Fulton, 1965) in which every death is regarded as due to the evil, magical machinations (evil eye, for example) of some other human being. Everyone is caught up in a paranoic madness related to the theme of death. This madness is not radically different from the kind we encounter in many schizophrenic patients who have elaborate delusions about other people trying to kill them. There are observers who have been so impressed with how often the schizophrenic assumes he is going to be lethally eliminated that they have theorized that fear of death plays a major part in serious psychological breakdown. It is probably accurate to say that themes of death exceed all others in the delusions of the psychotic. This is an important lead that has not received the study it deserves. Is it possible that many schizophrenic breaks are triggered by the overwhelming realization that death is inevitable and that the prized body will cease to exist? Does such an alarming realization lead to a delusional defense in which the threat of death is divorced from the natural scheme of things and instead directly tied to the intent of a malevolent person? If death can be redefined as due to the bad behavior of another human being, no matter how wicked, it is more tolerable than if it is the unavoidable outcome of a vast natural system. You can conceivably fight back against those who have human form.

In the course of working with schizophrenic patients I have been impressed by their preoccupation with fantasies of rebirth. The reminiscences of recovered patients about their periods of acute disturbance often depict them as times when profound inner transformation occurred, accompanied by the feeling that a new identity was being created. The Rorschach ink-blot images of these patients during their acute disturbance may focus on rebirth themes. Examples of such images are as follows: "caterpillar turning into a butterfly," "baby being born," "creation," "plant coming up through the ground." It is obvious that they could represent a mode of negating fear of death. It is also obvious that they are not different from the rebirth fantasies that typify many religious systems.

While it may be true that the child arrives at a fairly adult concept of death by the age of nine, there is also good evidence that he re-

tains many irrational and half-baked ideas about it throughout his lifetime. All sorts of irrational feelings may feed into his attitudes toward it.
One that should be spelled out relates to separation anxiety. People differ in how disturbed they become when separated from the people important to them. Mention was made in an earlier chapter of how frightening it was to Picasso in his childhood when he had to leave his father
to go to school. Apparently, he felt alone and deserted without his father's presence. It was also pointed out that later in life Picasso had
strong, irrational fears about death, and it was suggested that these
fears were derivatives of his long-standing sensitivity to the possibility
of being left all alone. His anxiety that members of his family might
die really meant that he feared that they might desert him. There is,
indeed, evidence that death and the act of hostile desertion are often
equated. With this perspective, it has been proposed that fear of death
is maximized in those who are most alarmed about being alone and the
possibility of losing relationships. They are so frightened by death because it conveys the possibility of losing those important to them, either through the others' death or through their own. An experimental
study has put this idea to the test. Ross (1966) measured both separation and death anxiety in nine-year-old children and found that when
he increased separation anxiety in them their death concern intensified.
In order to augment separation anxiety he employed a technique that
required the child to sit alone in a room for a period of time. Interestingly, when separation anxiety was increased it intensified death
concern more in girls than in boys.

We are only beginning to glimpse the influence of anxiety about
death upon our daily behavior. In studies that I instituted (Fisher,
1973) we discovered that concern about death (and the related fear
of losing loved ones) has a negative effect on a woman's ability to attain orgasm. We found that women with orgasm difficulties were likely
to be preoccupied with death imagery and fantasies of loss. When
asked to describe what a series of ink blots looked like, such a woman
produced a more-than-average quota of responses like "gravestone,"
"someone dead," "person killed," and "ghost." We also found an above-
average probability that she had lost her father early in life, especially
through his death. In the course of interpreting such data, we concluded
that the woman who is frightened about death and its related implications of losing important love objects finds the excitement stirred by
sexual stimulation to be threatening because it blurs her contact with
things and therefore makes her feel that she is "losing" them. It is well
documented that sexual excitement produces fuzziness in our percep-

tion of the outer world. Things become more vague and less articulated. In that sense, they become psychologically more distant, and to someone who is appropriately sensitive this phenomenon may be experienced as if it meant losing one's hold on objects. Thus, the woman who has grown up with the suspicion that relationships are not dependable (that significant figures in your life can be unexpectedly whisked out of sight by death) reacts with alarm to sexual arousal because it blocks clear perceptual contact, and this alarm, in turn, interferes with the ability to reach an orgasmic level of excitement. It is interesting that the French sometimes refer to orgasm as the "little death" because of the momentary dip in consciousness that it produces.

There is promising information to be gained in asking what other behaviors involving blurring of awareness are also affected by death anxiety. Swift movement through space may distort and attenuate your perceptions. The acceleration of an airplane or the whirling space capsule in the amusement park may act in this way. The same would be true of the quick twisting of your body while dancing or engaged in vigorous sports. Sensations of dizziness and the view of objects from unusual standing-on-your-head perspectives may predominate and impart an alien, less real quality to objects—as if they were "slipping away." Possibly, death anxiety keeps certain people away from activities that arouse such sensations because the feelings involved mean losing a hold on things as they are. Consider other related activities in which the same principle might apply. Would those with elevated death anxiety refrain from certain drugs or alcohol that diminish the clarity of consciousness? Would they avoid "mystical" reveries or hypnogogic states that call for moving away psychologically from real objects? This last question leads nicely into the issue of whether going to sleep, which means completely giving up your perceptual hold on the world, would not be especially alarming to the individual who fears death. There are popular metaphors in which death and falling asleep are compared. Some undertakers refer to the room in which the corpse is displayed as the "Slumber Room." A fair number of cases may now be found in the clinical literature in which persons with severe insomnia seemed to be preoccupied with the death implications of closing their eyes and ceasing to be conscious. To go to sleep was too uncomfortably analogous to what happened when you died. I know of one instance in which a young child who was in psychotherapeutic treatment for sleep difficulties, among other symptoms, openly verbalized the fear that when she went to sleep she could not be sure whether she would still be alive in the morning—or whether her parents would be. Sleep therefore had to be resisted. The assumption that there may be an equation of sleep and death is, of course, speculative and awaits scientific testing.

Life and death are tied to certain parts of the body more than to others. The genital organs, and especially the uterus, signify creation. But the heart is most often equated with living versus dying. If the heart is beating there is life. When it ceases to beat death has occurred. The fantastic psychological investment that each of us has in his heart has been highlighted in some of the tragic reactions to heart surgery. Even when such surgery is completely successful in relieving heart symptoms it often produces psychotic reactions that are difficult to explain. The psychological threat contained in the idea that someone is going to open your chest and do something to your heart is apparently of overwhelming force. Again and again this threat is more than the individual can tolerate, and his ego defenses break. He has to take refuge in unreal fantasies in order to deny what is happening to him. The average person is quite sensitive to the sensations in his heart. Even minor feelings of discomfort in that area evoke anxiety. The heart is especially prominent because it is really the only organ that constantly emits audible sounds. Its beat is always in the background and it is likely that we keep tuning in on it, sampling the rhythm to see if all is well. One writer (Schneider, 1954) speculates that you may feel driven by your own repetitive heart beat, as if it were racing you toward death. It is interesting, in this respect, that Poe, who was much preoccupied with death, showed a fascination with the heart in his literary productions. The beat of the heart in some of his stories sets a mood of tragedy and final destruction. Paradoxically, the heart beat is also linked with sexual excitement. The crescendo buildup of heart rate has obvious orgasmic associations. There are musical themes (as in Ravel's "Bolero") that make use of this equation by representing sexual arousal in a rapidly increasing drum beat, which sounds like the pumping heart. Perhaps it is not surprising that sexual excitement, which is, after all, a vehicle for the creation of new life, should be linked through the heart with the opposing concept of loss of life. The overlap between sexual and death images has been documented in studies involving the fantasies of dying women. It has been shown that such women may, in their imaginative stories, portray the figure of death as erotically attractive. Death may appear as a romantic lover rather than as a grim threat. McClelland (1963) has pointed out that death, in the guise of the Harlequin, has a long history of erotic connotations. Actually, there are cultures in which the funeral ceremonies become an occasion for promiscuous sexual intercourse (Fulton, 1965). Apropos of this general point, some psychoanalysts have proposed that dying may symbolically mean returning to Mother—to her womb. They note that burial means consignment of the body to Mother Earth. Several suicidal patients that I had the opportunity to study pursued death with a zeal that was amazing. They reached for death not in a despairing way but rather with the zest that is usually reserved for more positive, passionate affairs. I was also impressed with the rebirth images that some of them projected into their Rorschach ink-blot responses.

In time of danger some animals mimic death. They try to convince the predator that they are not worth attacking. Children, too, imitate the dead when they are playing. They may fascinatedly try out "dead" postures. Some funeral ceremonies have required relatives to inflict scars and other types of damage upon their bodies to represent metaphorically the damage to the dead one's body. Or it may be required, equivalently, that one's clothes be ripped. Case histories have been published that tell of persons who develop pains and body symptoms that exactly imitate those experienced by some loved one just before dying. It is as if an attempt were being made to identify one's body with that of the deceased. There are schizophrenic patients who model themselves after the dead in their catatonic stiffness. Such patients may also openly verbalize the delusion that they are dead. Or they may confine themselves to the belief that a limited sector of the body is dead (for example, the head, the "insides"). The conviction that a part of the body has died may be dramatically pursued by amputating it (sometimes without any overt signs of pain). Identification with the dead is floridly present in the person who attempts suicide or engages in dangerous activities that risk self-destruction. There are whole nations that have at times been caught up in a passionate involvement with death; to kill and be killed was a guiding motif. The time of the Nazi regime in Germany offers a good illustration.

How far should the average person go in trying on the "dead" role in preparation for growing old and eventually dying gracefully? To what degree is it good practice to explore the feelings and sensations of the dying so that the later decline of one's body will not be too alien in its impact? How can one get the feel of death in a way that will not be ego destructive? I doubt that there is a single best answer to any of these questions. If you scan the hundreds of different ways in which various cultures provide a knowledge of death and guide the individual into final acceptance of the decline of his body, you will be most impressed by their diversity. Quite opposite strategies may produce what look like equally workable adaptations. One culture may give the individual the vision that he need not concern himself with death because it is only a pause before moving on to a new resplendent existence; another may tell him that his death will be caused by sin and that there is a good chance he will have to suffer atonement in the Hereafter. What seems to be crucial is that he be given socially supported guidance in accepting the stages leading up to his demise. He has to hear in clear tones from the culture: "This is what dying means. This is how dying proceeds. Do not fear. Death is something that we all experience as part of our life role." It is pertinent to point out that one of the factors that was found to be crucial in maintaining morale in flight crews exposed to the constant threat of death in World War II was a sense of group unity. If the individual felt he was part of a cohesive group whose members were united in their struggle (against death?), he could usually cope with the danger of dying that faced him as an individual. In dramatic form this has been shown repeatedly in battles in which troop units advanced into certain death at a signal from a leader.

But how much should a person in our culture, as it now exists, concern himself with death? To what degree should he try on the feel of it in order to prepare himself for the end of his own life cycle? Is it good or bad to invest energy in pondering matters of death? While we have no direct information for coping with these questions, I would call your attention to some findings in a related area that are probably pertinent. Several studies have shown that when people are awaiting surgery, which obviously does have death implications, their overt degree of concern about what is going to happen to them predicts how well they will adapt psychologically to what is done to their body. But the relationship is not a simple one. It is the person who shows either very little or a great excess of concern about the surgery who is most likely to become seriously upset by it. The large middle group fares best. I would suspect that this will turn out to hold true also for concern about death. Those who either ignore the whole matter or who become highly preoccupied with it may eventually be least capable of coping with the imminence of dying. In any case, surveys that have shown that aged persons tend to have relatively low levels of death anxiety suggest that most people do gradually and adequately adapt to the concept that one's life terminates. The child reared in a "hothouse" atmosphere from which all traces of death are filtered out is at a disadvantage in coping with the threats that are bound to arise in this area. He does not have a chance to hammer out a workable concept of death. Portz (1964) demonstrated this empirically. He interviewed the parents of young children and obtained objective ratings of how open they had been about death. He also determined how much actual contact with death each child had had. Further, he obtained imaginative stories from the children both before and after an interview that was designed to arouse their anxiety about death. He discovered that the more open parents had been in giving information to their child about death and the more real contacts the child had had with death phenomena, the less disturbance he manifested when exposed to the stress interview dealing with death. The child who had been shielded from death found the interview to be disconcerting.

It is well known that when an average person loses a loved one because of death he subsequently goes through a difficult mourning period. He has to reconcile himself to his loss. It has been customary to attribute most of the disturbance during this period to the loss experience. However, I wonder whether we have underestimated the impact of the closeness of the look at death. If someone dies whom you know well, the reality of death is brought home with a vividness that is unique. You are suddenly unable to dodge the facts and must digest their implications with regard to your own career. Soldiers on the battlefield, who are called upon to live intimately and repeatedly with death, not infrequently become highly disturbed, even when those who perish are relative strangers. They have their noses rubbed in death, and they become hyperaware of its implications for their own existence.

Aside from the idea of dissolution and non-existence, what is there about the image of death that is so difficult to endure? I wonder if one of the basic elements of unpleasantness does not derive from something that has been found to be prominent in the young child's definition of death. He tends to equate death with a body that does *not move*, and when he imitates death it is the posture of being motionless that is central. If he moves a muscle, his playmates "shoot" him again. It is the idea that your dead body will cease to have the potentiality for voluntary intention that may be most disconcerting. This idea conjures up a picture of passivity that our entire adult career has been dedicated to preventing. To be a respected personage in the world you have to show that you can do things. You have to show that you can reach out and have an effect on your environs. You must have a certain minimum capability of taking care of yourself. Not to be capable of self-care means that you are reduced to the helpless child who cannot provide his own food and who is even incapable of controlling his body sphincters. The motionless body could also be the dirty body that fouls itself with its own feces and urine. For a man, the motionless body may be one that shamefully cannot defend itself against attack. It becomes the cowardly body. For a woman, the motionless body may signify shameful exposure to sexual indignities. She may equate inability to act with a surrender to sexual looseness. The specter standing behind death may be indecent helplessness.

Death carries with it the notion of confined space. The corpse is put into a box, which in turn is tightly squeezed into the earth. The motionless body could not move even if it were magically revived. In almost every culture there are fearful tales about being accidentally buried alive. A surefire way for a horror story to arouse distress is to describe the struggles of a victim who awakens to find himself buried in a casket. Death means being put into a compartment barely big enough to hold you. The claustrophobic reactions of many when they enter an elevator or go into a small basement room may be incited in part by the death implications of putting one's body into such a small chunk of space. The metaphorical similarity to the casket may be too intense to tolerate. Relatedly, those who always want to be on the move, out in the open, may be reassuring themselves that they are in no danger of being buried. It is not fully recognized how prevalent are fears of small spaces. I have found in discussions with psychiatric patients and also normal persons that almost everyone experiences some alarm when he finds himself being squeezed into a small area, even when there is no apparent rational reason for concern. There are a hundred situations that can be discomforting. Here are some common examples: being in a building that has no windows, going into a dark closet, entering a bank vault, visiting an underground cave, squeezing through a pipe in an obstacle course, going up a narrow stairway, driving through a tunnel. I am suggesting that such situations may symbolically call up images of what it is like to be the motionless, confined body. Those with a special sensitivity to death anxiety may find a good deal of provocation in the overcrowding of our cities and the regulated fenced-in character of city space. We have all had irrational fear surge over us at some time when we were standing in a huge city crowd that had our body "locked in." It is basically true that the more we have learned to apply technology to dividing and compartmentalizing space the more we have created situations in which the individual can perceive analogies to the closed-in burial arrangement. But let me add that, as was mentioned in an earlier chapter, some people also find the squeezed-in sensation to be comforting. They feel protected and guarded when they are closely enclosed. We must consider the possibility that the image of burial may, in these terms, be attractive to them. Or at least one can say that they are both drawn to, and repulsed by, the image.

The fact that people commit suicide has been difficult to fit into any of our accepted concepts of human motivation. Self-destruction violates our notions about self-preservation. It does not make sense that someone would destroy his dearest possession. Theories about suicide have ranged from assuming the existence of an instinct for self-destruction to complex models involving the turning of blocked hostile impulses inward against the self. I will not attempt to evaluate these theories, but I do think that an adequate explanation of suicide has to cope with the paradox that the individual annihilates an object of great worth that belongs to him. The explanation I would offer is that by the time someone tries suicide he no longer perceives his body as belonging to himself. Instead, he sees it as having become the bad possession of some outside person or force. I would theorize that those who are susceptible to suicide were raised by parents who early made them feel that they only partially owned their own bodies. Parents could accomplish this by such strategies as rarely permitting privacy, using the child's slight illnesses as an excuse to overcontrol physical activities, demanding perfectionistic sphincter control, arbitrarily requiring that certain kinds of clothes be worn (even if the child disliked them), and so forth. In this atmosphere a person might grow up with the sensation of having only a partial lease on his own body. Large sectors of his frame might seem to belong to his parents, and these sectors would have negative, unfriendly connotations to him. Given this sort of body perspective, it might take only a few crucial traumatic experiences later in life finally to convince the individual that his body did not at all belong to him but rather was an alien pain-producing partner of some other entity. He might work hard to gain recognition in some organization (a corporation, for example) and find that he had been "taken over" by its demands and no longer really had much to say about living his own life. He might develop cancer and regard his body as "taken over" by the pathological process. He might set up an intensely dependent relationship with a woman and gradually feel that she had "taken him over." There are endless ways in which people can be made to feel that they have lost genuine ownership of self and are occupied by hostile others. This is especially true if they are already susceptible to such feelings. When the individual concludes that his body is no longer his own and has become the domicile for hated forces, it is not so strange that he should want to attack and even destroy it. But so strong are the bonds of ownership that even in the very act of self-destruction many suicides seem to be concerned that they not disfigure the body too badly. Thus women, who presumably place more value than men do on an attractive appearance, are less likely to use suicide methods that would grossly disfigure them. Note that there is a general tendency for suicides not to use procedures that are grossly mutilating. At the last moment they adopt the same protective attitude toward the body that the culture does when it puts the corpse into a casket that will preserve it in the ground.

In everyday life how do we go about reassuring ourselves that we are safe from death? What other things do we do besides avoiding contact with the dying and clinging to religious belief that assure us of immortality?

Each of us manufactures a chain of realistic and semimagical procedures for safeguarding our health and preventing potentially life-threatening illness. We become dependent on the consistent observance of certain acts to reassure us that we are adequately protecting ourselves. These may include such diverse activities as eating three daily meals (each at a specific time), ingesting vitamins, having a bowel movement at a fixed point each day, exercising "sufficiently," lying under a sun lamp, not drinking coffee before going to sleep, getting a certain amount of fresh air, and so forth. The repeated hooking together of a series of such acts helps to create the illusion that one is actively defending oneself against serious illness. It counters feelings of passive vulnerability to whatever nature may want to dish out. In some ways, it functions like a daily prayer for good health.

Probably the chief strategy we use in reassuring ourselves against death is to conceal signs of aging. As the individual moves beyond his early 30s he becomes hypersensitive to evidence that he is growing old. He spots each gray hair and incipient wrinkle that appears. Aided by the best technology the culture can muster, he begins a campaign of camouflaging the stigmata of his decline. This technology is indeed effective, and a skillful woman can keep herself looking ten years younger than her true age. It is important to emphasize that such camouflage needs to be maximally effective when the individual confronts his own mirror image. The real test comes when he scans his reflection and concludes, "I don't look too old." While it is, of course, important to conceal aging from others, it is doubly so to keep the unpleasant news from himself. One of the natural safeguards against being overwhelmed by aging is the fact that it occurs gradually. The day-by-day increments of small changes may be assimilated without awareness of how they add up. But periodically there is an accounting when you meet an acquaintance whom you have not seen for a long time who betrays in his reactions that he perceives a large disparity between the you of today and the you of yesterday. Sometimes the individual arrives at a similar realization on his own when he compares current and earlier pictures of himself. This must occur often with popular figures such as movie actors who are much photographed and who cannot avoid seeing in vivid technicolor how they used to look. Some of the balky and illogical behavior that people show when others want to take pictures of them may represent a defensive attempt to avoid eventually being confronted with printed evidence of where they stand in the life cycle.

Still another defense against death is provided by quasi-merging with someone younger. It is an axiom that we live on through our children. We comfort ourselves that our offspring will carry on where we leave off. They are our extensions into the future. There is a metaphorical immortality in the succession of the generations. I would suggest that the inclination of many parents to take possession of their child's body may represent an attempt to become one with a younger chassis. By closely identifying with his offspring's body, especially as it blossoms during adolescence into the ideal young adult form, the individual can combat his sense of aging. He sees a young version of himself and he gets reassurance from his feeling that he has proprietary rights over it. However, if the adolescent resists being owned and emphasizes his difference from, rather than similarity to, his parents, this may lead to a dramatic contrast between the young and the old. We have not yet even begun to explore the extent to which conflicts between the adolescent and his parents stem from parental jealousy of the youthful body and the desire to establish some sort of partnership with it. Perhaps, more generally, some of the tension between the old and the young stems from their disturbing messages to each other about the nature of the life cycle. The old feel deteriorated in comparison with the young and envy their greater distance to death; the young resent this envy and also are disturbed by the intimations of mortality that they glimpse in the battered frames of their elders.

Maintenance of sexual prowess is still another way of proving that one has not yet moved too far down the road. Adequate sexual performance may become more a badge of functional youthfulness than a means of real gratification. Each sexual contact beyond middle age may, for some, be a micro-test of vigor. Not to be able to perform adequately is significant not so much as a sexual thing in itself but as a

sign of decline. This raises the question of whether the feverish preoccupation with sexuality in our culture is not, at least in part, a defense
against death fantasies. To be absorbed by the sexual is to focus on
the kind of excitement and creative potential that is the antithesis of
the image of the motionless body. I have seen disturbed individuals
who, in an attempt to stave off despair that did ultimately end in death
or psychosis, embarked on a period of intense and promiscuous seeking
of sexual adventure. Similarly, there are anthropological reports of
cultures that use mass sexual encounters in a ceremonial way at times
of crisis—drought, planting of new crops, etc.—to ward off potential
disaster.

It is informative and amusing to analyze the properties that we assign to our after-death selves. Probably the most typical of the post-bur-
ial forms is the ghost. The ghost lacks solidity. It is gaseous, without
weight, and capable of moving freely through matter. Walls and barriers cannot stop it. But at the same time it retains recognizable human
shape. It can even speak with its former live voice, although a few
eerie overtones are added. The most novel thing about the ghost is the
interpenetrating way in which it interacts. It lacks firmness or palpabil-
ity, but all other objects also lack the firmness to keep it out. In other
words, the ghost is an image of a "body" that is not terribly different
from a real one, except for the way in which it can merge with, and
flow through, other objects. We are so accustomed to the ghost concept
that we do not realize what a unique attribute this "merging" and
"flowing through" represents. While at one level it may merely symbol-
ize the idea of nonexistence, I wonder if it does not represent a widely
cherished and secret body-image fantasy. In our ghost myth we are
able to create a version of the body that can magically do something
we ordinarily cannot but wish we could. The ghost body can become
part of anything else. No object can ward it off when it wishes entry.
This paradigm sounds familiar. It is the core of the concept of symbiosis. It is an abstract statement of how the very early relationship between child and mother is often pictured. Presumably, the child initially feels fused with the mother. He can tap into her body whenever
he pleases (by sucking the breast), and she also taps into his in the
process of caring for it. All through the early years the psychological
attitude is maintained that the child's body and those of his parents are
permeable to each other. Dependence and symbiosis tend to foster
fantasies of interconnection that defy the usual laws of object separation. The ghost is a symbol of super symbiosis and in that sense may
reveal a fundamental belief that death leads to a reinstatement of what

was true in the early days of contact with one's mother. There are related ideas implicit in religious myths about the dead merging with God.

It has been pointed out that death marks off a limit to your life. No other factor so decisively declares that your existence is anchored in flesh and blood. You can't really outlast your body. I think insufficient attention has been given to the democratizing implications of this fact. No matter how glorious the fame of any person in the culture, both he and others are aware that there will be an end to it all. He will ultimately prove to be composed of the same materials as the average citizen. The cycle of the body is a leveler, and I would guess that many get a secret satisfaction out of hearing that a renowned personage has succumbed to the same somatic deficiencies that plague everyone else. Perhaps even more importantly, each individual may find the limits imposed by his body's mortality to be a significant restraint on his own grandiosity. No matter how high his success takes him, he cannot avoid at least a subliminal awareness of where he stands in the life-death sequence. This will tend to keep him human and less expansive. However, there are probably instances in which the individual cannot face up to the limitations mortality imposes on his concept of himself, and he falls back on compensatory, pathological brands of grandiosity. There are people who have had to pretend to themselves that they are Godlike and impervious to death. But in the eyes of others this is a pathetic expression of fear. Overall, I cannot find that serious effort has been invested in exploring how the fact of death shapes each person's concept of himself. Different patterns of personality are probably affected in different ways by the realization that one's life has an end point. Obviously, the effects would vary, too, at different stages depending on how close the individual felt he was to death. Consider some illustrative possibilities. A man who has grown up with the feeling that he is small, inferior, and vulnerable may react to his first clear perception of death with an even greater conviction of futility. He may conclude that there is no reason to strive or struggle. Another, upon clearly discerning the fact of death, may be impressed with the great power of natural processes and try to make his style of life fit with the larger aspects of nature. He may acquire an intensified sensitivity to the importance of his body in his existence and therefore live more by the cues and feelings emanating from his frame. Still another may let the fact of death frighten him into disowning his body. He may retreat to an ascetic position that abolishes body needs, with the hope that this will help to defend against death, which must strike through bodily channels. Another person may find in the image of death a rationalization for unlimited self-release and even removal of all self-control over aggression. If the end is death, why not simply do as you please? Enjoy yourself while you can.

I am certain that we will eventually find that the facts of death have different implications for the male and the female, but at this point one can only ask some logical questions. Is it possible that the female may be relatively less threatened by death because she feels more secure about her body than the male? Does the male find the implications of death more thwarting because he has greater dedication to the image of himself as an aggressive heroic figure who eventually wins out over life's odds? It is the male hero in myths who is most often fighting it out with death so that he can reach a prized goal. I have already mentioned the surprising finding that women may see in death not a threat but rather an erotic partner. The passivity explicit in the act of dying may link up with the passive elements in the feminine role that traditionally have sexual meaning. For a long time, sexual response in the female has been associated with submission to someone stronger. Consider, too, that the average woman is more accustomed to seeing drastic changes in her body, such as those resulting from menstruation and pregnancy, than is a man. This may render the idea of drastic corporeal alteration due to death less overwhelming.

Day by day we find some things more evocative of death than others. Sickness and body disablement are obvious examples of some with strong death significance. The sight of extreme aging has an analogous meaning, as does the passing away of a close friend. I have already mentioned the subtle equation that we make between death and someone's departure. When a loved one leaves on a trip this may stir up a childlike anxiety that going away means dying. But what other even less obvious occurrences momentarily get us whipped up about death? Consider the following, which I cite at random. A fleeting memory from your childhood may suddenly remind you how long ago that was and define where you now stand in the life cycle. The completion of a long and arduous task may confront you with the fact that all things have a beginning and an end. Submission to a demand that is compelling and unavoidable may metaphorically tell you there are inexorable forces that can seize you lethally. The racing of your own heart may conjure up a realization of how dependent you are on it for survival. Even the setting of the sun may, if you are in a properly sensitive mood, suggest the finale of being. The world is full of potential cues about dying. It is difficult to say how many register on us. What quantities of energy do we have to invest in denying and repressing them? The fact that a basic sensitivity to them exists has been well illustrated in studies requiring people to give associations to words that refer only indirectly to death. Although such people seem not to be consciously aware of the death connotations of the words, they do reveal definite signs of disturbance in their physiological responses.

The central place of death stimulates people to "practice" it by means of opportunities that present themselves in their own bodies. As they explore what it is all about, they try looking at disturbances in their own body processes as miniature death situations. For example, one person may feel a new, somewhat strange pain and ask himself, "What if this is an early sign of cancer?" Another may perceive a few heart palpitations and confront himself with the idea that he might be developing a serious, life-threatening, heart disease. A woman whose menstrual bleeding goes a few days longer than usual may ponder the likelihood of the presence of devastating uterine pathology. In each instance, the individual has a chance to savor fear of death in a well-diluted form. There is an opportunity to see how intense the fear gets and to experiment with techniques for controlling it. The individual can scan his own fantasies and calibrate the extent to which images of death permeate his interpretations of things in general. He can tell himself that he is afflicted with death and yet not believe it. He can toy with lethal possibilities and reverse them. To be able to play with a reversible image of death can eventually prove to be of real defensive value—in future situations where the lethal potentialities become serious. By being repeatedly wrong about the death implications of things that go wrong in his body he can dispute the inevitability of dying. Also, he gets an opportunity to appraise himself in direct, but miniature, brushes with death. Over the years he may repeat these encounters many times and gradually build up confidence in his ability to cope with dying. As he grows older, he also gets a related kind of practice in the course of experiencing the signs of body decline associated with aging.

The perception that death signals nonexistence is in itself sufficient to disconcert people. What is doubly disruptive is the fact that the theme of death gets hooked to a lot of other confusing and threatening issues. Consider a few of the connotations of death, aside from the literal meaning. It signifies loss of loved ones and also the act of deserting them. It means being afraid and yet escaping from all further difficulties. It calls up all sorts of conflicts about the existence of God and the practicality of immortality. But what is probably the most disturbing side issue is that death is linked to anger and aggression. There is a stage in the child's development when he can think of death only in terms of violence. People die because they are shot, stabbed, or exposed to other varieties of mayhem. Death is not a natural event. This child's view of death hangs on. We all, to an extent, equate death and aggression. So, when an adult person discovers he is in danger of dying he may become deeply concerned with translating his dilemma into terms of hostility. He may not be able to shake an underlying conviction that he would not be dying unless he were the victim of massive evildoing on someone's part. This attitude is indirectly reflected in the responses of many who suffer catastrophic or disabling accidents. Although their hurt is accidental, they become preoccupied with guilt feelings; they verbalize the idea that they must have committed serious misdeeds in order for something so terrible to be inflicted upon them. Why else would fate be so hostile and cruel? The person faced with death becomes similarly caught up with the feeling that he is the victim of an attack. He feels hated and in return he hates. Death becomes irrationally identified with personal hostility rather than with a natural cycle. If the hostility could be taken out of dying, much of the anxiety usually associated with the process might be eliminated.

References

Abram, H. S. 1970. "The Prosthetic Man." *Comprehensive Psychiatry*, 11: 475–81.

Anthony, S. 1940. *The Child's Discovery of Death*. New York: Harcourt Brace Jovanovich, Inc.

Apfeldorf, M. 1953. "The Projection of the Body Self in a Task Calling for Creative Activity." Unpublished doctoral dissertation, University of North Carolina.

Arnaud, S. H. 1959. "Some Psychological Characteristics of Children of Multiple Sclerotics." *Psychosomatic Medicine*, 21: 8–22.

Bethke, C. S. 1968. "Ethnic Responses to a Modified Clothing TAT." *Journal of Home Economics*, 60: 350–55.

Bullock, A. 1962. *Hitler, A Study in Tyranny*, Rev. ed. New York: Harper and Row.

Burian, R. J. 1970. "The Relationship between Female Body Physique and a Number of Psychosexual-social Correlates." Unpublished doctoral dissertation, Arizona State University.

Burma, J. H. 1959. "Self-tattooing among Delinquents." *Sociology and Social Research*, 43: 341–45.

Cantril, H., and Allport, C. 1933. "Recent Applications of the Study of Values." *Journal of Abnormal and Social Psychology*, 28: 259–73.

Cassell, W. A., and Hemingway, P. 1970. "Body Consciousness in States of

Pharmacological Depression and Arousal." *Neuropharmacology,* 9: 169–73.

Centers, L. and Centers, R. 1963. "A Comparison of the Body Images of Amputee and Non-amputee Children as Revealed in Figure Drawings." *Journal of Projective Techniques and Personality Assessment,* 27: 158–65.

Chessick, R. D. 1960. "The Pharmacogenic Orgasm in the Drug Addict." *Archives of General Psychiatry,* 3: 545–56.

Cleveland, S. E. 1956. "Three Cases of Self Castration." *Journal of Nervous and Mental Disease,* 123: 386–91.

Comer, R. J., and Piliavin, J. A. 1972. "The Effects of Physical Deviance upon Face-to-Face Interaction: The Other Side." Presented at the annual meeting of the Eastern Psychological Association, Boston.

Compton, N. H. 1964. "Body Image Boundaries in Relation to Clothing Fabric and Design Preferences of a Group of Hospitalized Psychotic Women." *Journal of Home Economics,* 56: 40–43.

———. 1962. "Personal Attributes of Color and Design Preferences of Clothing Fabrics." *Journal of Psychology,* 54: 191–05.

Crawley, E. 1931. *Dress, Drinks, and Drums.* T. Besterman, editor. London: Methuen & Co.

Cross, J. F., and Cross, J. 1971. "Age, Sex, Race, and the Perception of Facial Beauty." *Developmental Psychology,* 5: 433–39.

Douvan, E., and Adelson, J. 1966. *The Adolescent Experience.* New York: John Wiley & Sons.

Fast, G. J., and Fisher, S. 1971. "The Role of Body Attitudes and Acquiescence in Epinephrine and Placebo Effects." *Psychosomatic Medicine,* 33: 63–84.

Fisher, S. 1970. *Body Experience in Fantasy and Behavior.* New York: Appleton-Century-Crofts.

———. 1973. *The Female Orgasm: Psychology, Physiology, Fantasy.* New York: Basic Books.

———. 1964. "Power Orientation and Concepts of Self Height in Men: Preliminary Note." *Perceptual and Motor Skills,* 18: 732.

Fisher, S., and Cleveland, S. E. 1968. *Body Image and Personality.* New York: Dover Press.

Fisher, S., and Fisher, R. L. 1960. "A Projective Test Analysis of Ethnic Subculture Themes in Families." *Journal of Projective Techniques,* 24: 366–69.

Fisher, S., and Greenberg, R. P. 1972. "Selective Effects upon Women of Exciting and Calm Music." *Perceptual and Motor Skills,* 34: 987–90.

Fisher, S., and Osofsky, H. 1967. "Sexual Responsiveness in Women: Psychological Correlates." *Archives of General Psychiatry,* 17: 214–26.

Fisher, S. H. 1958. "Mechanisms of Denial in Physical Disabilities." *Archives of Neurology and Psychiatry,* 80: 782–84.

Frazier, J. G. 1959. *The New Golden Bough.* Abridgment by H. Gaster. New York: Criterion Books.

Freud, S. 1924. *Psychoanalytische Studien uber Werke der Dichtung und Kunst.* Vienna.

Fulton, R. (ed.). 1965. *Death and Identity.* New York: Wiley.

Gellert, E. 1962. "Children's Conceptions of the Content and Functions of the Human Body." *Genetic Psychology Monographs*, 65: 293–405.

Gillin, J. 1951. *The Culture of Security in San Carlos*. New Orleans: Tulane University Press.

Gilot, F., and Lake, C. 1964. *Life with Picasso*. New York: McGraw Hill.

Goffman, E. 1963. *Behavior in Public Places*. Glencoe, Illinois: The Free Press.

Goodman, M. 1964. *Race Awareness in Young Children*. New York: Collier Books.

Green, J. H. 1960. *Black Like Me*. New York: New American Library.

Greenacre, P. 1958. "The Relation of the Imposter to the Artist." *The Psychoanalytic Study of the Child*. New York: International Universities Press, pp. 521–40.

———. 1955. *Swift and Carroll*. New York: International Universities Press.

Himmelstein, P. 1964. "Sex Differences in Spatial Localization of the Self." *Perceptual and Motor Skills*, 19: 317.

Hitler, A. 1939. *Mein Kampf*. English translation by James Murphy. London: Hurst and Blackett.

Hollender, M. H. 1970. "The Need or Wish to be Held." *Archives of General Psychiatry*, 27: 445–53.

Holzman, P. S., Rousey, C., and Snyder, C. 1966. "On Listening to One's Own Voice: Effects on Psychophysiological Responses and Free Associations." *Journal of Personality and Social Psychology*, 4: 432–41.

Horney, K. 1959. *New Ways in Psychoanalysis*. New York: W. W. Norton & Co.

Jacobson, E. 1959. "Depersonalization." *Journal of the American Psychoanalytic Association*, 7: 581–610.

Jesser, C. J. 1971. "Reflections on Breast Attention." *Journal of Sex Research*, 7: 13–25.

Kagan, J., and Moss, H. A. 1962. *Birth to Maturity*. New York: Wiley.

Katcher, A. 1955. "The Discrimination of Sex Differences by Young Children." *Journal of Genetic Psychology*, 87: 131–43.

Katcher, A., and Levin, M. 1955. "Children's Conceptions of Body Size." *Child Development*, 26: 103–10.

Kaufman, L., and Heims, L. 1958. "The Body Image of the Juvenile Delinquent." *American Journal of Orthopsychiatry*, 28: 146–59.

Kernaleguen, A. P. 1968. "Creativity Level, Perceptual Style and Peer Perception of Attitudes toward Clothing." Unpublished doctoral dissertation, Utah State University.

Kovel, J. 1970. *White Racism*. New York: Pantheon Books.

Kubie, L. S. 1965. "The Ontogeny of Racial Prejudice." *Journal of Nervous and Mental Disease*, 141: 265–73.

Laing, R. D. 1959. *The Self and Others*. London: Tavistock Publications.

Lane, R. W. 1966. "The Effect of Preoperative Stress on Dreams." Unpublished doctoral dissertation, University of Oregon.

Lee, D. 1959. *Freedom and Culture*. New Jersey: Prentice-Hall.

Liebert, R. S., Werner, H., and Wapner, S. 1958. "Studies in the Effect of Lysergic Acid Diethylamide." *Archives of Neurology and Psychiatry*, 79: 580–84.

Lippman, C. W. 1952. "Certain Hallucinations Peculiar to Migraine." *Journal of Nervous and Mental Disease,* 116: 346–51.

McClelland, D. C. 1963. "The Harlequin Complex." *The Study of Lives,* ed. R. White. New York: Atherton, pp. 94–119.

———. 1964. "Wanted: A New Self-image for Women." *The Woman in America,* ed. R. J. Lifton. Boston: Houghton Mifflin, pp. 173–92.

McClelland, D. C., and Watt, N. F. 1968. "Sex-role Alienation in Schizophrenia." *Journal of Abnormal Psychology,* 73: 226–39.

McDonald, M. 1970. *Not by the Color of Their Skin.* New York: International Universities Press.

Nagy, M. H. 1953. "Children's Conceptions of Some Bodily Functions." *Journal of Genetic Psychology,* 83: 199–216.

Nash, H. 1958. "Assignment of Gender to Body Regions." *Journal of Genetic Psychology,* 92: 113–15.

Nichols, D. C., and Tursky, B. 1967. "Body Image, Anxiety, and Tolerance for Experimental Pain." *Psychosomatic Medicine,* 29: 103–10.

Peto, A. 1959. "Body Image and Archaic Thinking." *International Journal of Psychoanalysis,* 40: 1–9.

Piaget, J. 1929. *The Child's Conception of the World.* New York: Harcourt Brace Jovanovich, Inc.

Pitcher, E. G., and Prelinger, E. 1963. *Children Tell Stories—an Analysis of Fantasy.* New York: International Universities Press.

Poll, S. 1962. *The Hasidic Community of Williamsberg.* New York: Free Press of Glencoe.

Popplestone, J. A. 1963. "A Scale to Assess Hyperchondriasis: The Converse of Hypochondriasis." *Psychological Record,* 13: 32–38.

Portz, A. T. 1964. "The Meaning of Death to Children." Unpublished doctoral dissertation, University of Michigan.

Reitman, E. E., and Cleveland, S. E. 1964. "Changes in Body Image Following Sensory Deprivation in Schizophrenic and Control Groups." *Journal of Abnormal and Social Psychology,* 68: 168–76.

Roach, E., and Eicher, J. B. 1965. *Dress, Adornment, and the Social Order.* New York: Wiley.

Roe, A. 1951. "A Psychological Study of Eminent Biologists." *Psychological Monographs,* 65: 1–68.

———. 1953. "A Psychological Study of Eminent Psychologists and Anthropologists, and a Comparison with Biological and Physical Scientists." *Psychological Monographs,* 67: 1–85.

Rose, G. J. 1963. "Body Ego and Creative Imagination." *Journal of the American Psychoanalytic Association,* 11: 775–89.

Rosenzweig, S., and Shakow, D. 1937. "Mirror Behavior in Schizophrenic and Normal Individuals." *Journal of Nervous and Mental Disease,* 86: 166–74.

Ross, R. P. 1966. "Separation Fear and the Fear of Death in Children." Unpublished doctoral dissertation, New York University.

Rubin, I. M. 1967. "Increased Self-acceptance: A Means of Reducing Prejudice." *Journal of Personality and Social Psychology,* 5: 233–38.

Rudofsky, B. 1947. *Are Clothes Modern?* Chicago: Paul Theobald.

Sabartes, J. 1948. *Picasso, an Intimate Portrait.* Englewood Cliffs, New Jersey: Prentice-Hall.

Schachter, S. 1967. "Cognitive Effects on Bodily Functioning: Studies of Obesity and Eating." *Neurophysiology and Emotion,* ed. D. C. Glass. New York: Rockefeller University Press, pp. 117–44.

Schilder, P. 1935. *The Image and Appearance of the Human Body.* London: Kegan, Paul, Trench, Trubner and Co.

Schneider, D. E. 1954. "The Image of the Heart and the Synergic Principle in Psychoanalysis (Psychosynergy)." *Psychoanalytic Review,* 41: 197–215.

Schneider, S. C. 1960. "Analysis of Presurgical Anxiety in Boys and Girls." Unpublished doctoral dissertation, University of Michigan.

Stein, M. E. 1956. "The Marriage Bond." *Psychoanalytic Quarterly,* 25: 238–59.

Tait, C. D., Jr., and Archer, R. C. 1955. "Inside-of-the-body Test: A Preliminary Report." *Psychosomatic Medicine,* 17: 139–48.

Tausk, V. 1933. "On the Origin of the Influencing Machine in Schizophrenia. *Psychoanalytic Quarterly,* 2: 519–56.

Traub, A. C., and Orbach, J. 1964. "Psychophysical Studies of Body Image. I. The Adjustable Body-distorting Mirror." *Archives of General Psychiatry,* 11: 53–66.

van Lennep, D. J. 1957. "Projection and Personality." *Perspectives in Personality Theory,* ed. H. P. David and E. Von Bracken. New York: Basic Books, pp. 259–77.

Wapner, S. 1960. "An Experimental and Theoretical Approach to Body Image." Presented at Sixteenth International Congress of Psychology, Bonn, Germany.

Wapner, S., and Werner, H. 1965. "An Experimental Approach to Body Perception from the Organismic-developmental Point of View." *The Body Percept,* ed. S. Wapner and H. Werner. New York: Random House, pp. 9–25.

Wax, M. 1957. "Themes in Cosmetics and Grooming." *American Journal of Sociology,* 62: 588–93.

Williams, J. E. 1964. "Connotations of Color Names among Negroes and Caucasians." *Perceptual and Motor Skills,* 18: 721–31.

Wittreich, W. J., and Radcliffe, K. B., Jr. 1955. "The Influence of Simulated Mutilation upon the Perception of the Human Figure." *Journal of Abnormal and Social Psychology,* 51: 493–95.

Wolfenstein, M. 1954. *Children's Humor.* Glencoe, Illinois: The Free Press.

Wolff, W. 1943. *The Expression of Personality.* New York: Harper.

Index

173